POVERTY

ABOUT CANADA

POVERTY

Jim Silver

FERNWOOD
PUBLISHING

HALIFAX & WINNIPEG

Editing: Curran Faris
Design: John van der Woude
Printed and bound in Canada by Hignell Book Printing

Published in Canada by Fernwood Publishing
32 Oceanvista Lane, Black Point, Nova Scotia, BOJ 1BO
and 748 Broadway Avenue, Winnipeg, MB R3G 0X3
www.fernwoodpublishing.ca

Fernwood Publishing Company Limited gratefully acknowledges the financial support of the Government of Canada through the Canada Book Fund and the Canada Council for the Arts, the Nova Scotia Department of Communities, Culture and Heritage, the Manitoba Department of Culture, Heritage and Tourism under the Manitoba Publishers Marketing Assistance Program and the Province of Manitoba, through the Book Publishing Tax Credit, for our publishing program.

Library and Archives Canada Cataloguing in Publication

Silver, Jim, 1946-, author
About Canada : poverty / Jim Silver.

(About Canada series ; 10)
Includes bibliographical references and index.
ISBN 978-1-55266-681-4 (pbk.)

1. Poverty—Canada. 2. Poor—Canada. 3. Canada—Economic policy. 4. Canada—Social policy. 5. Neoliberalism—Canada. I. Title. II. Title: Poverty. III. Series: About Canada series; 10

HC120.P6S55 2014   362.50971   C2014-905175-1

CONTENTS

To our newest grandson,
the wonderful Odin Silver

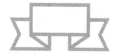

ACKNOWLEDGEMENTS

I am happy to acknowledge the many people I have had the privilege of working with on poverty-related issues over many years. I am particularly grateful to those that I have worked with in Winnipeg's inner city, especially at Lord Selkirk Park and the Selkirk Avenue education hub, but in numerous other inner-city projects as well. There are too many to name, and if I start I will surely miss some of you. Thanks to all of you for your friendship, your dedication and your hard and skillful work. I am grateful as well to the many wonderful people at the Canadian Centre for Policy Alternatives–Manitoba and the Manitoba Research Alliance, and I want in particular to thank Shauna MacKinnon, Lynne Fernandez, Elizabeth Comack and John Loxley, from each of whom I have learned a great deal and who have been a constant source of support over the years we have worked together.

I want to acknowledge the specific and excellent research support of Matt Rogers, with whom I have worked on previous research efforts. Thanks Matt.

I am pleased to acknowledge the generous financial support of the Social Sciences and Humanities Research Council of Canada through the Manitoba Research Alliance grant titled Partnering for

Change — Community-Based Solutions for Aboriginal and Inner-City Poverty.

Once again, I am pleased to acknowledge the support of all of the people at Fernwood Publishing involved in this project, Beverley Rach, Curran Faris and especially my good friend Wayne Antony, for their work on this book and their continued support of my work. Thanks also to John van der Woude for designing the cover of this book.

Most importantly, thanks to Loa Henry, my partner in all things for many years, for her ongoing love and support.

FORMS OF POVERTY

I t has often been said that poverty will always be with us. Perhaps it will. I don't think it need be. In a country as wealthy as Canada, we could largely eliminate poverty if governments and the citizens who elect them were to choose to do so. Eliminating or at least dramatically reducing poverty is a matter of political will. Rates of poverty in some industrialized countries—the Nordic countries in particular—are very low, while those in other industrialized countries—Canada for example, and especially our neighbour the United States—are very high. This suggests the possibility that different ways of doing things—different societal arrangements, different public policies—produce different levels of poverty.

That poverty need not always be with us is further suggested by the fact that in some societies there has been no poverty at all. Thomas Berger quotes a French Jesuit writing about the Iroquois in 1657:

> No hospitals [poorhouses] are needed among them, because there are neither mendicants or paupers as long as there are any rich people among them. Their kindness, humanity, and courtesy not only makes them liberal with what they have, but causes them to possess hardly anything

> except in common. A whole village must be without corn,
> before any individual can be obliged to endure privation.[1]

Some might argue that there was no poverty in such societies because everyone was poor. This would represent an especially narrow and limited understanding of poverty—one that sees poverty as simply a shortage of money and of the commodities that money can buy. Yet Mohawk society, including all of its members, was rich—not poor—in many fundamentally human ways. Poverty is often about more than a shortage of money.

What exactly is poverty, then? There are important debates in Canada about how to *measure* poverty, and in the next chapter I will describe the various positions in these debates. But the differing positions in these debates all revolve around poverty as being a shortage of money. I will argue that, as important as money is in a monetized society such as ours in Canada, there are forms of poverty that are about more than a shortage of money. Poverty is often complex, and multi-faceted, and can damage the human spirit in ways that are profound.

THE POVERTY CONTINUUM

I will break up the concept of poverty into two broad categories: the poverty related "only" to a shortage of income, and that which is more complex, including a multitude of factors that worsen poverty's impact. These should not be thought of as two airtight and mutually exclusive categories. Rather, they are better considered as a matter of degree, or as existing on a continuum, with poverty as a shortage of income, often a temporary phenomenon that may not cause lasting damage to those who experience it, at one end of the continuum—a student whose income is relatively low during her years at university, for example—and at the other end of the continuum is poverty as a more complex, multi-faceted, long-term and even intergenerational phenomenon that includes a shortage of money but much more and produces great damage to those who experience it.

When we think of poverty as a shortage of income it is useful to differentiate between absolute poverty and relative poverty. Absolute poverty occurs when people have so little money that they cannot acquire the bare necessities of life. This is not the most common form of poverty in Canada, although it certainly does exist—think of Canada's many homeless people, sleeping on the streets or in crowded shelters—and when it does, it produces many of the negative consequences associated with what I am describing as complex poverty. Relative poverty, by contrast, occurs when people's income is such that they can acquire some or most of the bare necessities of life, but are excluded from anything resembling a "normal" life.

Poverty at the other end of the continuum, complex poverty, exists when people experience not only a shortage of income, but also a

The Case of the Disappearing Shopping Carts

What shopping carts become in the hands of poor people:

- Moving vans for people who can't afford to rent
- Laundry transport, instead of big unwieldy garbage bags, with two kids in tow
- Wheelchairs and walkers—even Handi-Transit isn't free
- Emergency hospital transport for those who can't afford a $300 ambulance
- Recycling collection vehicle to earn income

(Adapted from Joy Eidse, 2010, "Poverty and the alternative uses of shopping carts," January 27, Winnipeg: CCPA-MB. <policyalternatives.ca/publications/commentary-youth-voices-poverty-and-alternatives-uses-shopping-carts>.)

host of other causally connected problems that can trap them in a cycle of poverty. These may include inadequate housing, poor nutrition and poor health, elevated exposure to crime and violence, low levels of educational attainment, intergenerational exclusion from the labour market and reliance on forms of social assistance, negative interactions with various agencies of the state—such as the police, the justice system, child welfare agencies, schools—and so on.

This complex poverty has grown in urban centres in North America and Europe, especially in the past thirty to forty years and is partly the product of global economic changes and the "retreat of the state" that are associated with the rise of neoliberalism. Often this poverty is racialized and spatially concentrated in urban centres—elsewhere I have called this "spatially concentrated racialized poverty."[2] Its complexity and deep-rootedness is such that although we *could* solve it, there are no quick or easy solutions.

POVERTY AND JOBS

A central theme of this book is that poverty of all kinds is in large part a function of people's relationship to the labour market. Those who are unemployed are at high risk of being poor because of a shortage of income, and generally speaking, the higher the levels of unemployment, the higher the levels of poverty. Those who are employed in the rapidly growing "precarious" labour market—jobs that are part-time, short-term, low-wage, non-union and without security and benefits—are also likely to be poor because of a shortage of income. They have jobs, but the jobs don't pay enough, and/or they aren't able to get enough hours. Throughout the twentieth century, these kinds of poverty have risen and declined in tune with the ups and downs of the always-cyclical capitalist economy. If the capitalist economy is in recession, more people are wholly or partly out of work and thus are poor, insofar as having a shortage of income; if the capitalist economy recovers and begins to grow again, jobs are created and many such people are employed, and their wages or salaries lift them back out of poverty. For many poor people, poverty is thus not a life-long experience, but rather is something that they experience for a short period in their lives. In these cases, the poverty that results is not as likely to be associated with the range of inter-related negative factors identified above as being part of complex poverty, and is not as likely to produce lasting social and psychological damage to those who experience it—although it *may* be. Complex poverty, especially spatially concentrated racialized poverty, is often long term, because people caught in this kind of poverty have much greater difficulty entering the labour market, even if jobs *are* available.

CHILDREN, FAMILIES AND THE REPRODUCTION OF POVERTY

A second theme of this book is that a central feature of complex poverty and its reproduction is its effect on children. The term "child poverty" can be misleading in that children are poor because their families are poor, and in that sense, child poverty is actually family poverty. The structure of families has changed rather dramatically over the past thirty to forty years, and different types of families—the numbers of parents or caregivers and especially of children—are associated with varying levels of poverty. But the notion of child poverty as such is nevertheless useful because we know that poverty, and especially complex poverty, can damage and disadvantage children in a wide variety of ways, resulting in the children of poor families being much more likely to end up being poor themselves. And perhaps worse, growing up in complex poverty can significantly increase the likelihood of a range of adverse consequences. For example, there is a wealth of evidence that children in poor families are less likely to succeed in school, are more likely to experience poor health, are more likely to be apprehended by child welfare authorities, are less likely to secure good jobs when they reach working age and are more likely to be in trouble with the law and to end up being incarcerated. These and other similar adverse consequences of complex poverty contribute to the reproduction of poverty. It therefore follows that if large numbers of children in Canada are poor because they are living in families that are experiencing poverty—especially complex poverty—then we, as Canadians, are creating a host of problems that will manifest themselves in the near future and will be costly, financially and otherwise, to everyone.

SOME OTHER TYPES OF POVERTY

Within these two broad categories of poverty—poverty as a shortage of income that may be temporary and may cause no lasting damage to those who experience it, and poverty that is more complex and typically more long-term and damaging—there are many other variations. Poverty of the elderly, for example, has historically been a problem. Once people were no longer working in the paid labour force because of their age, they had insufficient income to support themselves and they experienced poverty. This problem was largely solved in most advanced industrial economies in the 1960s and 1970s because of government-introduced pension schemes that raised the incomes of retirees above the poverty line. In 1961, the poverty rate for senior families was almost double that of younger families; in 2008 it was a mere 1.6 percent.[3] Recent changes in Canada—changes that are consistent with neoliberalism—may have the effect of pushing more seniors back into poverty.

Certain regions of Canada are more likely to have significant numbers in poverty. This has historically been the case in Atlantic Canada, for example, because of the character of the labour market there—i.e., the relative lack of well-paid jobs. The same has been the case in Canada's north, and especially on First Nations reserves. Indeed, poverty in Canada is increasingly racialized—disproportionate numbers of Aboriginal people and non-white newcomers are poor, and this is likely to continue to be the case since these categories of people are among the most rapidly growing in Canada.

Women have been more likely than men to be poor (this is the phenomenon known as the feminization of poverty) partly because women have historically been more likely to be confined to the home and excluded from the paid labour force, and partly because when in the labour force, women have been paid less, on average, than men. The rise of single parenthood has accentuated the feminization of poverty because the sole responsibility for the care of young children keeps single women out of the labour force, or confines them to low-paid, part-time jobs, and because government support systems have eroded with the rise of neoliberalism.

THE COMPLEXITY OF POVERTY

There is a wealth of statistical data about poverty. But while statistical analyses are useful for some purposes, they are limited by the disagreement about how much money one needs to rise above poverty and about what actually constitutes poverty. Most statistical analyses focus only on poverty as a shortage of income and as a result cannot offer much of a glimpse into lives lived in the context of complex poverty. Thus the statistical approach to poverty misses much. Nevertheless, an analysis of poverty by the numbers can tell us certain important things. It can show the trend in levels of poverty over time, for example, so that we know whether poverty—however measured—is rising or falling or staying much the same. It can show that poverty affects certain parts of the population more than others. For example, the incidence of poverty is related not only to one's relationship to the labour market, but also to the structure of one's family. Single-parent families are more likely to be poor than two-parent families; families with two partners in the paid labour force and no children are rarely poor. Statistical data can also provide evidence that poverty is racialized and gendered and has a spatial dimension. These are all useful in furthering our understanding of the nature of poverty in Canada.

Poverty has been affected by the dramatic economic changes of the past thirty to forty years. During this period we have seen a big change in the character of the labour market, with the relative

Claudette and Bingo

"Because bingo is a ways and means of life here in the North End. I won $30.00 last night, that's how I got my teabags, wieners and buns and mustard, these things are extras I can't afford on Frank's and my welfare. Things other people take for granted. I haven't had a cup of tea in two months! You won't believe how good that tea tasted! Now that I have $5.00 from the money Lynne gave me and $5.44 from my bingo win.... You know what bingo means to me? It means financial freedom if I win really big. I'd be off welfare. We can take care of ourselves. It would be a whole new world."

— *Claudette is a 45-year-old Aboriginal woman who lives in Winnipeg's North End. She and her husband are unable to work because of health problems.*

Source: Jil Brody, with CLOUT and Angelica, Allen, Claudette, Janette, Sabrina, Hannah and Taryn, 2009, It Takes All Day to Be Poor: State of the Inner City Report, 2009, Winnipeg, CCPA-MB

decline of full-time, permanent jobs that are unionized and pay a wage sufficient to support a family, and the corresponding relative rise of "precarious" jobs, or jobs that are part-time, non-permanent, not unionized and do not pay enough to support a family. In the same thirty to forty year period, we have also seen the relative reduction in governments' expenditures on a wide variety of social services. These two inter-related phenomena are often referred to as neoliberalism, and among neoliberalism's many consequences has been persistently high levels of poverty and significantly growing levels of inequality, giving rise to increasing levels of complex poverty.

Complex poverty in Canada, especially its urban form, is typically spatially concentrated and racialized. This can be seen, for example, in many public housing complexes where it is typically the case that a high proportion of residents, all located in one small geographic space, have poverty-level incomes, are on social assistance and are of Aboriginal descent or are racialized newcomers or non-Caucasian. Such poverty is associated with a wide range of social problems that go well beyond a shortage of income. The poverty experienced by these communities is more likely to be long lasting and even intergenerational, and it often causes deep psychological damage to those who experience it. In fact, this kind of poverty often damages the human spirit and erodes peoples' sense of self-worth, instilling a sense of hopelessness about their future that makes it so difficult to get out of this form of complex poverty.

Along with the personal spiritual damage, poverty is very expensive socially and economically. Poverty is associated with poor educational outcomes, poor health outcomes and a greater likelihood of involvement with the criminal justice system and of incarceration. And each of these produces a cost that is borne by society as a whole. It is widely known that health care is costly; poverty is a

Janette's Pride

"It's all about pride. I want my son to work for a living, not sit on welfare...and live off of welfare that way. Be proud, work for what you want. Growing up...I didn't ever know what welfare was. There's no pride being on it and they (workers) seem to think everyone on welfare is lazy. Not true! I'd pick up garbage or do almost anything just for a pay cheque with my name on it. Show my son with some hard work he could have the world... Welfare gives us $387 for rent, my rent is $525. So $138 comes out of our food budget. We haven't had cable or a phone for over a year."

—Janette is a Black woman who grew up and still lives in Winnipeg's North End with her 10-year-old son

Source: Jil Brody, with CLOUT and Angelica, Allen, Claudette, Janette, Sabrina, Hannah and Taryn, 2009, It Takes All Day to Be Poor: State of the Inner City Report, 2009, Winnipeg: CCPA-MB

major driver of health care costs. When the children of the poor do less well in school—and almost all studies suggest, on average, that this is the case—they are less likely to be employed, or employed in a well-paid job, when they reach adulthood and are therefore less likely to be producing the tax revenue that society as a whole needs. When such children get in trouble with the law, as is more often the case for those living in complex poverty, the costs of incarceration are high. Poverty is sufficiently costly that however much it might cost to dramatically reduce poverty—and dramatically reducing complex poverty would be especially expensive—doing so is nevertheless likely to be more cost efficient than to continue to bear the large societal costs that poverty produces.

Given the huge social and economic costs, it makes sense to consider what kinds of things might be done to significantly reduce the incidence of poverty in Canada. The argument that will be advanced is that we know what to do to reduce poverty significantly. There are solutions that are known to work—investment in early childhood development, investment in the production of enough low-income housing units to meet demand and the promotion of trade unions, which can negotiate wages and benefits that will support families, for example. But Canada and Canadians lack the political will to spend the money and make the legislative changes needed to implement these solutions over an extended time. It is not necessarily the case that poverty will always be with us, but Canadians and our elected governments would have to acquire the political will to implement a range of policies that would, over a generation or so, produce enormously positive effects on Canada's poverty problems. While doing so is distinctly possible, it would be quite inconsistent with the dominant neoliberalism of our times and with the economic interests of that powerful minority who derive benefits from the dramatic growth of income inequality in recent decades. For poverty in Canada to be dramatically reduced, some significant changes in government policy would have to be made; and for that to happen, significant numbers of Canadians would have to organize themselves in order to *demand* that such changes be made. Poverty is largely the result of political choices—choices about policies and about broad ideological orientations, for example. Eliminating poverty, or at least dramatically reducing it, will require putting pressure on governments so that different political choices are made.

POVERTY BY
THE NUMBERS

We can learn much about poverty by analyzing various quantitative data. In particular, a quantitative approach can yield insight into the temporal and spatial incidence of poverty — that is, are poverty rates going up or down over time and are they higher in some countries and in some regions of a country than others? Also, a quantitative analysis can yield insight into what kinds of people are most likely to be poor. These characteristics are important to know if we are to make sense of poverty.

On the other hand, there are limits to what quantitative data can tell us. In particular, a focus on the numbers too often implies that poverty is only about a shortage of money. Much of Canada's poverty is what I will call "complex poverty," which includes a range of other interacting problems beyond a shortage of income.

THE POVERTY LINE

There is endless debate about what the poverty line is. Several versions are used in Canada. The after-tax low-income cut-off (A/T LICO) is used most often. Other options include the low-income measure (LIM) and the market basket measure (MBM).

The LIM is typically used for making international comparisons because the method is fairly simple: the threshold for low income or poverty is 50 percent of the median income, adjusted for family size.

The MBM includes a calculation of actual expenditures on shelter, food, clothing, transport and other basic household needs to produce a "modest, basic standard of living," using a reference family of two adults and two children.[1] Adjustments are made for family size and for costs in varying geographic locations. A family, of a particular size and in a particular community, experiences low income or poverty if their actual income is not sufficient to purchase this basket of essentials. This measure depends, of course, on just what is and is not included in the "basket." The MBM often produces a higher rate of poverty than the A/T LICO.

Even though the A/T LICO is the most frequently used measure of poverty, Statistics Canada, which produces the data, does not call it a measure of poverty. They call it a measure of low income. With the A/T LICO, the low-income threshold is reached when a family spends 20 percent more of its after-tax income on food, clothing and shelter than the average family. Adjustments are made to accommodate seven different family sizes and five different ranges of community population, resulting in thirty-five different A/T LICOs. For example, a family of four living in a community of 30,000 people would have a different A/T LICO than a family of three living in a city of 1.2 million people. The base year for this calculation is 1992, in which year the average family spent 43 percent of its after-tax income on food, clothing and shelter. Those households that spend 63 percent (20 percent more than the average family) or more of their income on these three essentials have low income, or are in "poverty." Although the A/T LICO is adjusted annually by the amount of the consumer price index, it is still calculated from the base year of 1992. It is thought that if the base year were to be brought up to date — if it were to be "re-based" — the result would be a higher incidence of low income/poverty. That is because it is generally believed that Canadians are now spending, on average, a smaller proportion of their incomes on food, clothing and shelter than they did in 1992. If, for example, the average Canadian family is now spending 40 percent of its after-tax income on the three essentials, rather than the 43 percent that was the case in 1992, then those below the A/T LICO would be spending 60 percent or more, as opposed to 63 percent or more, of their income on food, clothing and shelter. This would produce a larger number and a larger percentage of people — that is, the number of people spending 60 percent or more would be greater than those spending 63 percent or more — and thus the incidence of poverty as measured by the A/T LICO would be higher than currently shown.

There is no perfect measure of poverty. All measures are, at least in part, both arbitrary and relative as opposed to absolute measures. However, the A/T LICO is most commonly used in Canada, and past A/T LICO data are available, so this measure can be used to identify trends over time and to identify those groups of people more or less likely to experience low income or poverty.

POVERTY TRENDS IN CANADA, 1976–2011

The poverty trend line reveals several important things about poverty in Canada over the last thirty-five-plus years. First, the incidence of poverty tends to rise during recessions. It reached 14 percent in 1983 as the result of the recession of the early 1980s, then declined, and peaked again at just over 15 percent in 1996 following the recession of the early 1990s and the massive cuts in Federal Government social spending in the early-mid 1990s. Since 1996, the incidence of poverty has steadily declined, turning upwards only slightly in 2008 and 2009 as the result of the global economic crisis of 2007–8, and

Canada has been stuck at 3 million+ poor Canadians for thirty-five years.

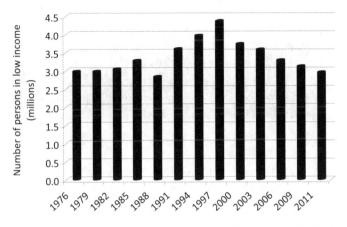

Source: Statistics Canada, Table 202-0802, Persons in low income families, annual, CANSIM [Database]

then resuming its decline in 2010–11. As measured by the after-tax low-income cut-off, the incidence of poverty in Canada was lower in 2011 than it had been at any time over the past thirty-five-plus years since 1976.

Why has the incidence of poverty, as measured by the A/T LICO, declined over the past fifteen years or so? There are several possible factors. First, rates of unemployment have declined over that period, and the incidence of poverty closely tracks the rate of unemployment: when unemployment rises, so does the rate of poverty; when unemployment declines, so does poverty. Poverty has a great deal to do with whether one has a job, what kind of job it is and how much the job pays.

Second, in 1997 the Federal Government introduced the Canada Child Tax Benefit (CCTB) and the National Child Benefit Supplement (NCBS), both aimed at reducing family and child poverty. The CCTB pays a fixed, tax-free amount per child to all parents; the NCBS

Unemployment and poverty go hand in hand

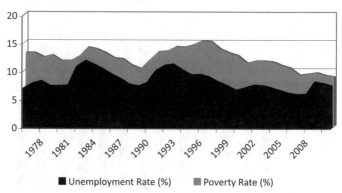

Source: Statistics Canada, Table 109-5324, Unemployment rate, Canada, provinces, health regions (2013 boundaries) and peer groups, annual (percent), CANSIM (database); Statistics Canada, Table 202-0802, Persons in low income families, annual, CANSIM [Database]

is an additional amount based upon income. The CCTB and the NCBS, together with the GST credit, have made it possible for large numbers of Canadians, and especially those with children, to move above the poverty line. Third, in some provinces—Manitoba is an example—taxes on very low-income people have been reduced in a variety of ways, and this is reflected in the lower incidence of the A/T LICO. Fourth, the real value of the minimum wage has increased in recent years in most provinces. Fifth, it may be that the poverty reduction plans (see Chapter 6) introduced in various provinces, with the exception of British Columbia and Saskatchewan, over the last decade or so, starting with Quebec's plan in 2002, are having an impact, although the data are not clear on this.

Or, it may be that A/T LICO is not really measuring poverty accurately and the incidence of poverty has not really been in decline at all. The incidence of poverty in Canada as measured by a different indicator, the after-tax low-income measure (LIM), has continued to rise in recent years. Why would there be a difference between the after-tax LICO and the after-tax LIM? There are several parts to any plausible explanation. First, there is no perfect definition or measure of poverty. Each measure is built upon different assumptions. Statistics Canada refers to "the imprecise and to some degree arbitrary operationalization of poverty concepts coupled with the statistical variability of surveys" and the essentially political nature of such estimates.[2] Second, the after-tax LIM likely reflects the growing gap between the rich and the rest of us (discussed later in this chapter) to a greater extent than does the A/T LICO, thus suggesting that inequality is growing worse in Canada. And third, the A/T LICO is calculated using a 1992 base year, as mentioned above. Expenditure patterns have changed since then, and it is generally believed that if the LICO were to be "re-based," it would show a higher incidence of poverty.

Even if the A/T LICO is the more accurate measure—and it may

Discrepancies in measuring poverty in Canada. Poverty rates depend on how they are measured; using the after-tax LICO, for example, has made poor people "disappear" in recent years

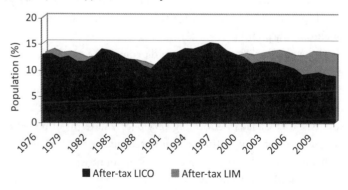

Source: Statistics Canada, Table 202-0802, Persons in low-income families, annual, CANSIM [Database]

or may not be, as suggested in the previous paragraph—it would be a mistake to conclude from the decline in the incidence of poverty that poverty is no longer a problem in Canada. Poverty is a major problem in Canada. The numbers of Canadians in poverty, that is, the numbers of people with incomes below the A/T LICO, are still high—just under 3 million in 2011. The "low-income gap" or "poverty gap" is large and has not declined in line with the decline in the incidence of poverty. The poverty gap represents the difference between a poor family's income and the LICO, expressed as a percent. If the LICO was, for example, $10,000, and a family's income was $7,000, the poverty gap would be $3,000, or 30 percent. In Canada, the poverty gap has fluctuated over a fairly narrow range, between about 30 percent in 1989 and almost 35 percent in 2005. This means that, on average, those households below the LICO are *well* below that poverty line. So, while the percentage of people at or below the poverty line may have declined in recent years, the depth of poverty and the level of inequality are high and stubbornly so. Further, a significant proportion of those who are poor in Canada remain in poverty for extended periods. As Rob Valletta, an economist who studies poverty trends puts it: "Canada has a high share of individuals always poor or chronically poor."[3]

Other countries, especially the Nordic countries, have much lower poverty rates than Canada. Dennis Raphael, a long-time poverty researcher from York University, shows that if we use the common international measurement, the low-income measure (LIM), the results show "Canada performing very poorly in terms of poverty ranking: 19th of 30 industrialized nations for adults, 21st for families with children, and 20th for children."[4] Four countries—Denmark, Finland, Sweden and Norway—have child poverty rates of 5 percent or lower, while Canada's is triple that, at 15 percent.[5]

People at Risk of Poverty

In Canada, particular groups of people are more likely than others
to be poor. One important determination is family type: single
mothers and unattached individuals are more likely to be poor than
are couples. In 2010, 20.6 percent of single mothers—one in every
five—had incomes below the poverty line. As high as this is, it is
important to note that it is less than half the level reached in 1996.
Unattached individuals experienced poverty rates ranging from
almost 12 percent to just under 35 percent, depending upon the
sex and age of the individuals. Rates for elderly married couples, by

**Single mothers and individuals are much more likely to be poor
than families**

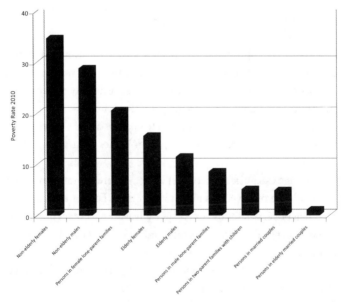

Source: Statistics Canada, Table 202-0804, Persons in low income, by economic family type, annual

Women have always been poorer than men

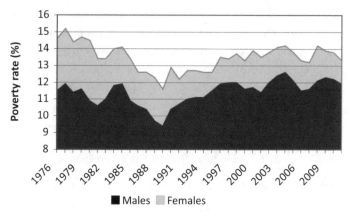

Source: Statistics Canada, Table 202-0804, Persons in low income, by economic family type, annual, CANSIM [Database]

contrast, were approximately 1 percent, while the average for two-parent families with children was 5 percent. The fact that some family types are more likely to be poor than others is largely a function of their differing relationships to the paid labour force.

Women are more likely than men to be poor. Since 1980, poverty rates for women have consistently been higher than poverty rates for men.

In all age categories except ages 45–54, where the rates are equal, the incidence of poverty is higher for women than for men, and the spread in poverty rates by sex is especially wide for older (65+ years) and younger (18–34 years) women and for racialized and Aboriginal women.[6]

This inequality in poverty rates occurs in part because of the lower wages earned by women. Social researcher Monica Townson found that 10 percent of men, but 20 percent of women, are in low-wage occupations, and in Canada, the gender gap is "among the highest in the world."[7] Women earn, on average, 71 percent of what men earn.[8] Approximately 60 percent of minimum wage earners in Canada are women; more than 70 percent of part-time workers are women.[9] As sociologist Pat Armstrong has put it: "The size and persistence of the wage gap clearly indicates that the problem does not stem from individual women and their capacities or from the practice of a few employers. ... Women as a group face a common set of practices that disadvantage them in the labour force."[10]

Young people, both women and men, have a relatively high incidence of poverty. For all family types, those under the age of 25 have a much higher incidence of poverty than do those 25 years and over.[11] Low wages are a particularly important factor, and this has been the case since the early 1980s. Low wages are in turn a function of the fact that young people comprise a large and growing proportion of

Canada Ranks 20th in Treatment of Women

The latest annual World Economic Forum's Global Gender Gap Report, which measures the rate of gender disparity between men and women in 136 countries, ranks Canada 20th and the United States 23rd. This is a drop by Canada from the 18th spot in 2012.... This report determines its findings across four primary areas: (1) economic participation and opportunity, (2) educational attainment, (3) political empowerment, and (4) health and survival.... The countries that ranked above Canada and the U.S., not surprisingly, were led by Iceland in top spot, followed by the Scandinavian nations Finland 2, Norway 3, and Sweden 4, countries that traditionally have scored highest in policies that promote gender equality.

Source: CCPA Monitor, *December 2013/January 2014, p. 3*

workers employed in precarious jobs—jobs that are part-time, low-wage, non-union and without benefits or job security. For those young workers without post-secondary education, it is worse: "less than one-quarter have full-time permanent jobs."[12] Economist Benjamin Tal finds that there is currently a record high number of youth who have *never* held a job, and he argues that without policy changes they are likely to remain chronically unemployed.[13] These young people face economic challenges unlike those of previous generations, and this trend has been developing over the past thirty years. Armine Yalnizyan, a senior economist with the Canadian Centre for Policy Alternatives (CCPA), has observed:

> People under 35 years of age are evidently worth less than workers of the same age before the recession of 1981–82. But it is the young men whose hourly rates of pay have been most sharply and consistently eroded over the past 15 years. Virtually every data source, from Census to special surveys, documents this same trend. Study after study shows that we are devaluing the young.[14]

In the period from 1981 to 2011, younger men experienced a reduction in their real wages—for men aged 17–24 years, between 13 and 14 percent, and for men 25–34 years, from 3 percent to a small gain of 1 percent. Older men experienced a net gain in real wages, ranging from 13 to about 20 percent. For women the trend is similar, although not as pronounced: younger women aged 17–24 years experienced reduced real income; women 25 years and older experienced real wage gains.

For younger Canadians, this relative loss of real purchasing power is made the worse when related to changes in housing prices. While

**Men's wages, especially those of young men, have declined quite
dramatically over the past thirty years.**

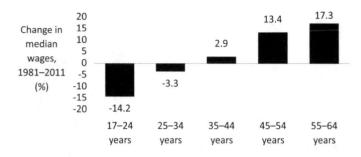

Change in
median
wages,
1981–2011
(%)

Source: Rene Morissette, Garnett Picot and Yuqian Lu, 2012, The Evolution of Canadian Wages over the
Last Three Decades, Ottawa: Statistics Canada

real incomes in Canada have remained relatively constant over the
period 1976 to 2011, residential housing prices have risen more than
six-fold. The growing gap between real incomes and housing prices
is striking.

Rising housing prices are more likely to accrue to the benefit of
older Canadians, who are more likely to be homeowners. They have
seen the value of their homes appreciate dramatically. For them, rising
housing prices are an advantage. For younger Canadians who may
want to start a family and own a home, however, these same gains
in the value of housing are a major disadvantage. Business journalist
Rob Carrick refers to Royal Bank of Canada data showing that "to
qualify to buy the average-priced two-storey home in Toronto and
Vancouver ... a couple would need gross annual household income of
$132,100 and $156,200, respectively." All across the country "houses
are being priced out of reach for first-time buyers and households
with income levels at or even a little above average."[15]

A similar pattern prevails with respect to university tuition, which

Change in Housing Prices
In Relation to Household Income (1976–2011)

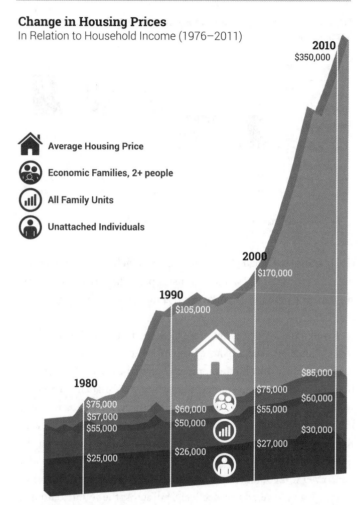

2010
$350,000

Average Housing Price

Economic Families, 2+ people

All Family Units

Unattached Individuals

2000
$170,000

1990
$105,000

1980

$85,000

$75,000

$75,000
$57,000
$55,000

$60,000

$75,000

$60,000

$55,000

$50,000

$30,000

$25,000

$26,000

$27,000

Source: Statistics Canada, Table 202-0603, Average after-tax income, by economic family type, 2011 constant dollars, annual (dollars); Canadian Real Estate Association, 2013, "Canada, average house price," Internal data, available upon request from CREA. All values approximate.

has risen far faster than real wages. Governments are reducing the share of universities' costs that they cover, meaning that students' tuition and other fees pay an ever-growing proportion of total university costs — an increase from 12 to 35 percent from 1979 to 2009.[16] This "downloading" of the cost of university from governments to students — typical of neoliberalism, as described in the next chapter — has meant a dramatic increase in tuition costs. For Canada as a whole, real income grew by 22.1 percent from 1990–2011, while total tuition and compulsory fees grew by more than ten times as much — 254.7 percent.[17]

Housing and education are two important means of establishing future security. Both are much more expensive today than in the past. Younger Canadians are particularly disadvantaged: their real wages are declining while the cost of housing and education is rising. As Angela MacEwen, economist with the Canadian Labour Congress, said when referring to young Canadians' difficult job prospects: "It's a pretty bleak picture for young people, especially when you factor in rising house prices and the high cost of tuition."[18] It would be reasonable to anticipate that this squeeze between reduced incomes and rising costs will lead to more poverty in the future.

Members of racialized groups—including Aboriginal peoples and other people who are non-Caucasian in race or non-white in colour—have a much greater chance of being poor. In 1996, the incidence of poverty for members of racialized groups was double that for the Canadian population overall.[19] By 2006, "Poverty rates for racialized families [were] three times higher than non-racialized families."[20] This is in large part because racialized Canadians are over-represented, relative to non-racialized Canadians, in low-paid jobs in the service sector — janitorial jobs and security service jobs, for example. This is the "colour coded nature of work" in Canada.[21]

One in three children in Ontario living in a racialized family is in poverty. In the Greater Toronto Area, while 10 percent of children of European ancestry live in poverty, the incidence of poverty increases to 20 percent for children in East Asian families, 33 percent for children in Arab and West Asian families and 50 percent for children of African families.[22] Further, racialized men and women are 24 and 48 percent more likely to be unemployed than non-racialized men, respectively, while racialized women earn, on average, 55.6 percent of what non-racialized men earn. These numbers are made particularly significant by the fact that in 2006 just over 16 percent of Canadians were part of a racialized group, and by 2031 "it's estimated racialized Canadians will make up 32 percent of the population."[23]

For Aboriginal people, rates of poverty are even higher. For example, according to 1996 Census Canada data, almost two-thirds—64.7 percent—of Aboriginal households in Winnipeg, home to Canada's largest urban Aboriginal population, had incomes below the poverty line.[24] In 2001, this number had declined to 54.7 percent—still over one-half of Aboriginal households in the city as a whole—while 71.3 percent of Aboriginal households in Winnipeg's inner city had incomes below the poverty line.[25] Across Canada in 2006, the median income for Aboriginal people was 30 percent lower than for the rest of Canadians. That gap has narrowed since 1996, but the rate at which Aboriginal people were catching up was such that "it would take 63 years for the gap to be erased."[26]

For Aboriginal people the problem of poverty becomes especially apparent when children are included. David Macdonald and Dan Wilson of the CCPA analyzed 2006 data and measured poverty via the LIM. What they found is that while 17 percent of all children in Canada live in families with incomes less than 50 percent of the median Canadian family income, the corresponding rate for Aboriginal children is 50 percent. In Manitoba and Saskatchewan—each of which has large Aboriginal populations—the rate of poverty for First Nations children was 62 and 64 percent, respectively.[27] These are appalling rates of poverty.

If we consider these three categories of people together—young Canadians, racialized Canadians and Aboriginal people—and extrapolate into the future, there are reasons for concern. Aboriginal Canadians constitute the youngest and the fastest growing demographic group in the country[28]; racialized Canadians comprised about 16 percent of Canada's population in 2006, but by 2031 they are predicted to be 32 percent of the population. Clearly, Canada's demographic makeup is changing dramatically. Both Aboriginal people and racialized Canadians, and especially Aboriginal and racialized children, experience very high rates of poverty. So if current trends continue unabated, the numbers of people in poverty and the incidence of poverty will grow in the future. And when we consider the circumstances of young Canadians generally, we see that their real wages are falling while the costs of establishing some security in life via housing and education are rising rapidly. This too causes concern for future levels of poverty. Recent declines in the incidence of poverty in Canada as measured by the after-tax LICO are no reason for complacency.

Food bank usage also reflects the continued need to be concerned about poverty. In March 2013, 833,098 people in Canada used food banks—more than the population of a relatively large city, such as Hamilton and Winnipeg, and more than twice the combined population of Regina and Saskatoon. The numbers of Canadians using food banks has doubled since March 1989 and grown 23 percent since 2008, following the severe economic crisis of 2007–8. And while children and youth represent about 21 percent of Canada's population, they comprised 36 percent of those using food banks in 2013.[29] At the beginning of the 1980s there was no such thing as a food bank in Canada. It speaks volumes about the problem of poverty that in a country as rich as Canada, we now take the existence of food banks for granted. And as Food Banks Canada explains it: "The key factor at the root of the need for food banks is low income," including people "working in low-paying jobs."[30]

POVERTY AND THE LABOUR MARKET

A person's relationship to the paid labour force is the most important determinant of poverty. This is also the case for families. Two-parent families and couples without children have the lowest incidence of poverty, mainly because they are most likely to have a second wage earner in the family—an option not available, by definition, to unattached individuals. Single-parent families have relatively high rates of poverty, largely because of the much greater likelihood that they will have no wage earners. A single parent with children under five years of age is more likely to be poor because of the obvious difficulty of going out to work in the paid labour force when the children are not yet in school, and also because of the shortage of childcare spaces in Canada. Racialized Canadians and Aboriginal people are more likely to be poor because they are more likely to be either unemployed or employed in a poorly paid job.

As long ago as 1996, Canada's precarious labour market was being described as "the main cause of persistent poverty."[31] People were working, but they were still poor. Since the mid-1970s, between 45 and 55 percent of low-income people of working age have had at least some earnings.[32] In 2008, approximately two-thirds of poor families in Canada had at least one family member in the paid labour force.[33] These are families of the working poor. Families are especially vulnerable to being among the working poor when the sole income earner is self-employed, or is working part-time or in a temporary job.

The growth of part-time jobs is an important factor connected to poverty. The proportion of jobs that are part-time grew steadily from under 5 percent in the 1950s to 19 percent by the early-mid 1990s. Since then the rate has stayed at about 19 percent—almost one in five employed Canadians. In the mid-1950s, one in twenty job opportunities in Canada was part-time; by the mid-1970s it was about one in eight; and by the mid-1990s and through to today, just under one in every five job opportunities in Canada is a part-time job. In clerical, sales and service occupations, six of every ten workers—60 percent—are part-time, a fact contributing to the relatively high proportion of people in those occupations who have incomes below the poverty line.[34] Part-time workers, on average, earn lower hourly wages than full-time workers and are less likely to be unionized and less likely to have access to a benefits package, which typically includes pensions, medical/dental coverage and paid sick leave, for example. Members of racialized groups, especially women, are over-represented in part-time, low-wage jobs—a major factor in their higher incidence of poverty.[35]

Taking a part-time job is often a matter of choice; but still, the percentage of part-time workers who wanted but could not find full-time jobs tripled between 1975 and 1994, from 11 to 35 percent.[36] In 2005, just over one-quarter (25.6 percent) of those working part-time did so because they were unable to find full-time work.[37] A study by Benjamin Tal found that in 2012 a record number of youth in the 15–19 and the 20–24 age groups were working part-time, and about 70 percent of them were "doing so involuntarily—meaning that they want to work full-time."[38] The result, described two decades ago and still fully accurate, is what social policy researcher Grant Schellenberg described as a "polarization of the work force—with one group of workers receiving good wages, benefits and job security, and another group, including most part-time workers, receiving poor wages, no benefits and little security."[39]

The same would be the case for temporary workers, a classification that has grown from 11.3 percent of all employees in Canada in 1997, to 13.6 percent in 2012. In that year there were just over 2 million Canadians in temporary positions in Canada. The growth in temporary employment is occurring primarily in the service sector, and a growing proportion of temporary workers are young people, especially in the 15–24 age category.

Self-employment also contributes to low incomes. The downsizing of corporations and layoffs of government employees have made self-employment not just an option but often a necessity for many people. From 1976 to 2012, the number of self-employed Canadians more than doubled, from 1.2 million to 2.7 million; their share of the total numbers of employed grew from just over 12 percent to just over 15 percent. Self-employed workers earn less than paid employees, such that in 2001 "the incidence of poverty was four times higher among the self-employed than among salaried workers."[40]

Low wages are an important factor in explaining poverty in Canada. In the twenty-year period from 1976 to 1995, the annual earnings of a full-year, full-time worker employed at the minimum wage declined by 25 to 30 percent in almost every Canadian province.[41] In the past decade, the national average minimum wage has increased, so that by 2010 it was almost back to the level it had reached in 1976, as expressed in 2010 dollars. Poverty researcher Ken Battle attributes this recent gain to the "growth of provincial and territorial poverty reduction strategies ... [which have] focused attention on the importance of minimum wages," but he cautions that "history shows that what goes up can later go down when it comes to minimum wages."[42]

CHILD POVERTY

A particularly troubling aspect of poverty in Canada is the growth of child poverty, the incidence of which is now about double that in most Nordic countries.[43] This is despite the decline in the incidence of child poverty in Canada, as measured by the A/T LICO, since its peak in 1996 — a decline largely attributable to the Canada Child Tax Benefit and the National Child Benefit Supplement, both introduced in 1997.

Despite this decline, child poverty in Canada is still far too high. It is high relative to other countries, and its long-term consequences are damaging. The Conference Board of Canada ranks Canada an abysmal fifteenth out of seventeen industrialized countries in the incidence of child poverty, and observes that "the failure to tackle the poverty and exclusion facing millions of families and their children is not only socially reprehensible, but it will also weigh heavily on countries' capacity to sustain economic growth in years to come."[44] Worse, we know that particular categories of children —those living in racialized and Aboriginal families, for example — experience much higher rates of poverty, and racialized and Aboriginal families are growing especially rapidly in Canada.

The notion of "child poverty" is misleading. The National Council of Welfare quite rightly observed almost two decades ago that "children are poor because their parents are poor."[45] The issue is poor families. Growing up in a poor family can severely harm a child's life chances. Researchers David P. Ross and Paul Roberts examined the correlation between family income and twenty-seven indicators and

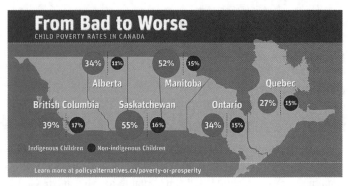

Source: *CCPA Infographic,* From Bad to Worse. *At* <policyalternatives.ca/publications/facts-infographics/
infographic-bad-worse-child-poverty-rates-canada>

found that children living in low-income families were "at a greater
risk of experiencing negative outcomes and poor living conditions
than those in higher-income families."[46]

Some of these correlations are striking. For example, delayed
vocabulary development occurs four times more frequently among
children from low-income families than among children from high-
income families; and "about one in six teens from low-income families
is neither employed nor in school, compared to only one teen in
twenty-five from middle- and high-income families." The result is
what Ross and Roberts call "poverty of opportunity." Children who
grow up in poor families are, on average, less likely to do well in life
than are children who grow up in non-poor families.[47]

Campaign 2000, which describes itself as "a national movement to
build awareness and support for the 1989 all-party House of Commons
resolution 'to seek to achieve the goal of eliminating poverty among
Canadian children by the year 2000,'" describes child poverty's lasting effects:

Child poverty is associated with poor health and hygiene, a lack of a nutritious diet, absenteeism from school and low scholastic achievement, behavioural and mental problems, low housing standards, and in later years, few employment opportunities and a persistently low economic status.[48]

In its 1975 study titled *Poor Kids*, the National Council of Welfare made much the same argument:

To be born poor is to face a lesser likelihood that you will finish high school, lesser still that you will attend university. To be born poor is to face a greater likelihood that you will be judged a delinquent in adolescence and, if so, a greater likelihood that you will be sent to a "correctional institution." To be born poor is to have the deck stacked against you at birth, and to find life an uphill struggle ever after.[49]

Consider this observation in light of the high incidence of poverty among Aboriginal children. In Manitoba and Saskatchewan, where there are large numbers of Aboriginal people, the rates of poverty for Aboriginal children are 62 and 64 percent, respectively. We know that educational outcomes for Aboriginal youth are lower than the population at large,[50] and that the prison system, especially in Manitoba and Saskatchewan, is populated to a wildly disproportionate extent by people of Aboriginal descent. As Elizabeth Comack observes:

Although Aboriginal people made up just 3 percent of the Canadian population in 2007–8, they accounted for 18 percent of admissions to provincial and territorial jails and 18 percent of admissions to federal prisons. This overrepresentation is most acute in the Prairie provinces. In Saskatchewan, Aboriginal people made up 11 percent of the population and a whopping 81 percent of provincially sentenced custody admissions in 2007–8. In Manitoba, Aboriginal people made up only 15 percent of the population yet represented 69 percent of provincially sentenced custody admissions.[51]

Poverty, especially when associated with racism and the lasting effects of colonialism, produces negative outcomes, including high rates of incarceration, which in turn contribute to the reproduction of poverty.

Poverty also has particularly adverse effects on health. International and Canadian health researchers point to what are called the "social determinants of health." If we ask, "Why are some groups of people healthier than others?" the answer has far less to do with biomedical and/or lifestyle factors (whether one smokes or is overweight or fails to exercise), than with *social* determinants. It is our living conditions—quality of housing, employment status, and especially poverty—that are particularly important factors in shaping health outcomes. Those who are poor are much more likely to suffer poor health.

We know too that poverty is about much more than a shortage of money, as important as that is in a money-based economy. The effects of poverty—and racism and colonization—are often internalized by those who are poor, resulting in a loss of self-confidence and an erosion of self-esteem, and in some cases even a sense of hopelessness about the future, a sense of being trapped.[52] This too produces adverse health and educational outcomes and contributes to the persistence of poverty in Canada. Children born into poverty, and particularly children born into complex poverty, are likely to experience many more difficulties and are much more likely to end up being poor themselves, than is the case for children who do not grow up in poverty. Child poverty matters.

THE PROBLEM OF INEQUALITY

Of importance to children's future health and education, and of importance to the quality of life of all Canadians, is the growing inequality experienced in much of the Western world, Canada certainly included, over the past thirty years or so. We have experienced a dramatically widening gap between the richest Canadians and the rest of us. While the real incomes of Canadians have remained almost constant over the past thirty years or so, the total wealth generated by the country, measured in constant dollars, has doubled.[53] The incomes of most Canadians are not growing in correspondence with the income of the country as a whole.

More than that though, there is a redistribution of income and wealth upwards, to the 10 percent and even 1 percent of the population who are the most well-off Canadians. Armine Yalnizyan examined the before- and after-tax earnings of Canadian families with children eighteen years and younger. She found that in 1976 the richest 10 percent earned thirty-one times what the poorest 10 percent earned; by 2004 that gap had almost tripled to eighty-two times. During that period, the bottom half of Canadians saw their real earnings decline — despite the healthy economy — while the earnings of the richest 10 percent grew by 30 percent. The 100 most highly paid Canadian CEOs "saw a 262 percent increase in compensation, pocketing an average of $9.1 million in 2005."[54] In 1998, they had earned 106 times what the average Canadian worker earned; in 2012 they earned a remarkable 171 times the income of the average

The Income Parade

In a one-hour parade where the height of the people marching is based on their income and wealth, the tallest and richest people would appear in the final moments of the parade. These people would be taller, and richer, when compared to royalty in England over three-hundred years ago.

Canada, 2007:
- At six minutes: tiny barely visible people (society's poorest)
- At 15 minutes: 3-foot people
- At 40 minutes: normal height (people with average incomes)
- At 50 minutes: seven feet or so
- At 54 minutes: 14-foot people
- At 59 minutes 50 seconds: people of 2000–8000 feet (the richest people in Canada, who would be taller than the CN Tower)

England, 1688:
- At 15 minutes: tiny people (vagrants, rogues, vagabonds)
- At 15–20 minutes: 2-foot people (servants, labourers)
- At 20–55 minutes: normal height (masons, blacksmiths, weavers, shopkeepers, innkeepers)
- At last few minutes: 50 feet tall (merchants and sea-traders)
- At last few seconds: 108 feet to 185 feet (armoured knights and bishops and archbishops [who proclaimed the poor/meek shall inherit the earth!])
- At last instant: 815 feet (aristocrats—kings, princes, dukes, earls and the like)

Source: Linda McQuaig and Neil Brooks, 2011, The Trouble with Billionaires, *Toronto. Penguin Canada, p. 11–13*

Canadian worker and 194 times the income of the average Canadian woman. Economist Hugh Mackenzie has calculated that the average member of the 100 highest-paid CEOs in Canada earned as much by about 1:00 pm on the first working day of 2012 (that is, in half a day) as was earned by the average Canadian full-time employee in the *entire* year. He adds that the average total compensation received by each of the 100 highest-paid CEOs in Canada in 2012 "would be enough to wipe out the budgetary deficits of any of the following provinces: Saskatchewan, Manitoba, Newfoundland and Labrador, New Brunswick, Nova Scotia or Prince Edward Island."[55] Yalnizyan concludes: "No previous generation of rich Canadians has taken such a large share of the gains of economic growth in recorded history."[56]

The same is the case for the distribution of wealth, as opposed to income: "All the gains of growth since 1980 have been received by the top 10 percent."[57] Yalnizyan concludes:

Only the richest 20% are experiencing gains from Canada's

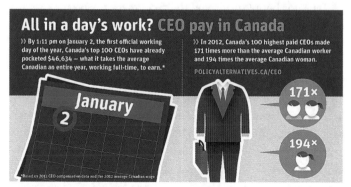

Source: CCPA, All in a Day's Work, *Infographic. At <policyalternatives.ca/publications/facts-infographics/ infographic-all-days-work>*

economic growth, and most of those gains are concentrated in the top 10%. The share of income going to the bottom 80% of Canadian families is smaller today than it was a generation ago, in both earnings and after-tax terms.[58]

More recently, it has been argued, "Income inequality in Canada is being driven by the richest 1 and 0.1 percent."[59] In 2010, there were sixty-one billionaires in Canada. They owned twice as much wealth as the approximately seventeen million Canadians in the bottom half of the income distribution.[60] In short, the resumption of strong economic growth in the late 1990s did not produce growth in the earnings of most Canadians; almost all of that growth accrued to the benefit of the richest Canadians.

Even greater inequality prevails in the U.S.: "In 1976, the top 1 percent of U.S. families held 19 percent of the country's wealth. By 2000, they held 40 percent of it,"[61] while by 2007 the top 10 percent of Americans earned almost 50 percent of income, "a level higher than any other year since 1917."[62]

Thus, for both Canada and the U.S., there has been a massive redistribution of income and wealth from most of the population to the very richest. The famous billionaire investor Warren Buffet is reported to have described this massive upward shift of income and wealth as a class war, and added, "but it's my class, the rich class, that's making war, and we're winning."[63]

The same trend has occurred in Quebec and Manitoba, although in both of these cases the gap has not widened as much as in Canada as a whole, primarily because provincial governments in those provinces have been somewhat more interventionist than the Federal Government. As will be seen, government spending is especially important for those at the bottom of the income scale.

What is striking is that this widening of the earnings gap, with declines at the bottom of the scale and stagnation for the majority of Canadians, has happened not during an economic downturn, as might be expected, but during what was an economic boom. Writing in 2007, before the economic crisis of 2007–8, Yalnizyan said: "In Canada, this is the best of economic times. Over the past decade, Canada's economy has consistently been firing on all cylinders," and yet "the gap between rich and poor families has risen in recent years at a rate not previously recorded ... at a time when the gap should be shrinking, not growing."[64]

This dramatic increase in the size of the gap between the rich and the rest of us is important because the social determinants of health literature, mentioned above, has shown definitively that a wide range of social ills—poor educational outcomes, poor health, a higher incidence of crime, for example—are a product not just of poverty but also of inequality.

Adding up the Numbers

What the quantitative analysis of poverty reveals is contradictory. On the one hand, the incidence of poverty in Canada is declining, at least as measured by the A/T LICO, although not as measured by the after-tax LIM. On the other hand, the quantitative data reveal many serious problems. For example, women continue to experience a greater likelihood of being poor than men, in large part because of their relatively disadvantaged relationship to the labour market. Also, young people and children in both racialized and Aboriginal families experience a much higher incidence of poverty than the population at large. In some cases—Aboriginal children, for example—the shockingly high incidence of poverty is shameful and completely unacceptable in a country as wealthy as Canada. This is especially important because, if it is young people generally, and the children of the fastest growing populations in Canada—racialized and Aboriginal people—who are experiencing the highest rates of poverty, we can anticipate a growth well into the future in the incidence of poverty and poverty-related problems. These problems can be complex and difficult—although not impossible—to solve. Yet, poverty is quite simply so costly—in financial as well as human terms—that it is a huge error for a country with Canada's wealth to allow it to persist. The direction that Canada has taken over the past thirty years is such that, in the absence of a significant redirection, poverty will not be solved, and the human and financial costs will continue to grow. This would be a shame, when a better way forward is possible.

NEOLIBERALISM
AND ITS EFFECTS

The incidence of poverty is directly related to the state of the economy. When the economy is strong and producing lots of good jobs, poverty levels drop; when the economy weakens and is not producing enough good jobs, poverty levels climb. This equation has been consistent over time, although today it is leavened by two things: the role that the state—the government—does or does not play in protecting Canadians against the inevitable ups and downs of the capitalist economy; and the structure of the economy, and especially the structure of the labour market — that is, the kinds of jobs being produced. The structure of the labour market is different in different parts of Canada, and thus poverty levels are different in different parts of Canada. But also, and more generally, the basic structure of the labour market has been changing dramatically in recent decades, as has the role of the state in the economy. These changes are associated with the increased economic globalization and the ideology and related set of policies typically referred to as neoliberalism.

Neoliberalism involves turning more economic decision-making authority over to the private sector, especially large corporations, and correspondingly reducing the role of the state—especially governments' social spending. Thus neoliberalism may take the form of privatization, deregulation, reductions in government expenditures, reduced levels of taxation and the introduction of measures that make it more difficult for Canadians, and especially lower-income Canadians, to receive various kinds of benefits, such as employment insurance, social assistance, social housing or retirement benefits. It is in these ways that neoliberalism typically leads to persistently high levels of poverty. As geographer Neil Smith observed: "Neoliberalism has been a long, difficult and violent ride for millions if not billions of people around the world," including Canada. It "has left behind, and continues to produce, a trail of human destruction."[1] Neoliberalism is just the most recent in the ever-evolving forms that capitalism takes, and thus the same could be said about capitalism, generally, as Neil Smith said about neoliberalism.

CHANGES IN THE ECONOMY OVER THE PAST THREE DECADES

The high levels of poverty throughout the 1980s and into the mid-1990s, shown in Chapter 2, were associated with the relatively weak economy during that period. As measured by almost every indicator, the Canadian economy—like virtually all economies in the industrialized world—was much weaker in the 1980s and first half of the 1990s than it had been during the long, post–Second World War economic boom. The average annual rate of growth in both gross domestic product (GDP) and employment from 1950 to 1980 was about double the rate from 1981 to 1997 and about triple the rate from 1990 to 1997. It is no surprise, therefore, that the incidence of poverty peaked at 16.2 percent, as measured by the after-tax LICO, in 1996. From 1998 to 2007, the rate of growth in GDP returned to levels close to those from 1950 to 1980, and the incidence of poverty dropped — but the rate of growth dropped again between 2008 and 2012 to its lowest level, largely attributable to the financial crisis of 2007–8. Unemployment rates from 1981 to 1997 were almost double the rates from 1950 to 1980 and remained almost half again as high from 1998 to 2007. This relative economic stagnation was reflected in the emergence of annual deficits and a buildup of accumulated debt from 1981 to 1997.

Why did the Canadian economy experience such a decline in the twenty-five years or so to the late 1990s? The character of the global economy is a partial explanation. The prevailing capitalist system has certain intrinsic features, chief among which is the constant, competitive drive of individual business firms to earn profits. This never-ending drive for ever more profits has certain inevitable results. One of them is a constant revolutionizing of the means of production, leading to rapid technological change, as firms relentlessly innovate in attempts to gain an advantage over their competitors. Another is the constant drive to expand, which results in both ever-larger firms and geographic expansion, as transnational corporations scour the globe in search of lower wages, bigger markets and cheaper raw materials in order to maximize their profits. One of the results of this process is that many manufacturing firms have left Canada in search of opportunities to make greater profits elsewhere in the world. Canada has lost, and continues to lose, many well-paid jobs as a result.

While economic activity has become much more global in the past quarter-century, globalization is not a new phenomenon. Rather, it is an accentuation of the drive to expand that is intrinsic to capitalism. In the past few decades, trade between nations and investment across national borders has increased dramatically. Companies do not confine their production to their home nations. They set up production facilities anywhere in the world, locating wherever they are most likely

A capitalist economic boom loses steam after the Second World War

	"Golden" age	Recession		Resumed growth	Economic crisis and recovery
	1950–1980	1981–1989	1990–1997	1998–2007	2008–2012
Average annual growth, real GDP (%)	4.7	3.1	1.8	3.3	1.1
Average annual growth, real GDP per capita (%)	2.8	1.9	0.7	2.3	-0.1
Average annual growth, total employment (%)	2.6	1.9	0.7	2.1	0.8
Average unemployment (%)	5.4	9.6	10.0	7.2	7.4
Change in government spending (% of GSP) [A,B]	18.5	4.3	-3.5	-5.9	2.4

	1950–1980	1981–1996	1997–2007	2008–2011
Annual federal deficit (% of GDP) [C]	0.3	-5.3	0.8	-1.9
Federal debt (% of GDP) [D]	23	53.1	44.9	32.7

Notes: A - All spending (federal, provincial, and municipal).

B - Data only avilable through 2011.

C - Annual federal deficit averaged over era.

D - Annual closing federal debt, averaged over the time period....

Sources: Jim Stanford, 1995, "The Economics of Debt and the Remaking of Canada," Studies in Political Economy 48: 113–35; Jim Stanford, 1999, Paper Boom, Ottawa: Canadian Centre for Policy Alternatives;

to maximize profits, "as transnational entities, corporations can play one nation off against another by moving to where the concessions and incentives are greatest, the relative labour costs lowest ... and environmental and employment standards the most limited."[2]

This trend has been accelerated by international trade agreements, such as the Canada-U.S. Free Trade Agreement and the North American Free Trade Agreement, and potentially the Comprehensive Economic and Trade Agreement (CETA), which is in negotiation as this book is being written. These trade agreements significantly reduce the capacity of elected governments to place limits on the profit-seeking activities of transnational corporations (TNCs). Trade agreements free these corporations from many of the "obstacles"—what most of us would look upon as benefits, such as environmental regulations and labour standards—formerly imposed on corporations by governments. Such changes increase the freedom not of individual citizens, but of TNCs—this is where the "free" in free trade comes from: TNCs are freed from government restrictions. This makes it easier for them to scour the globe in search of the most profitable production sites, making it more likely that the corporations will set up shop wherever they can maximize their profits. This is especially the case for heavily unionized, relatively high-wage, mass-production industries. According to political economist Gary Teeple, "The effects

World Bank, 2013, "Canada," World DataBank—World Development Indicators; Statistics Canada, Table 282-0002—Labour force survey estimates (LFS), by sex and detailed age group, annual (persons unless otherwise noted); Statistics Canada, Table109-5324—Unemployment rate, Canada, provinces, health regions (2013 boundaries) and peer groups, annual (percent), cansim (database); Statistics Canada, Table 380-0030—Gross Domestic Product (GDP) and Gross National Product (GNP) at market prices and net national income at basic prices, annual (dollars), cansim (database); Statistics Canada, National Income and Expenditure Accounts: Data Tables, catalogue number 13-019-X; Government of Canada, 2012, Fiscal Reference Tables, Ottawa: Department of Finance.

of this emerging global labour market began to become visible from the early 1970s on with a general downward pressure on wages in the industrial world."[3]

CHANGES IN THE CHARACTER OF CANADIAN JOBS

In the face of the intensified competition created by globalization, companies have sought not only to reduce wage levels, but also to create what the corporate sector calls more "flexible" workforces. Corporations have sought to move away from the relatively fixed and permanent high-wage regime characteristic of the mass-production industries of the 1950s and 1960s—sometimes called "Fordism," after the mass-production, relatively high-wage system introduced early in the century by Henry Ford—to a more flexible labour force, increasingly characterized by employment that is part-time, low-waged, non-union and without benefits or job security—what I referred to in the preceding chapter as "precarious labour." Examples of this are the growth in part-time and temporary employment and in self-employment.

Another example of "flexibility" is the Canadian government's policies in recent years promoting the use of temporary foreign workers, which, like the shift to a more flexible labour force in general, has had the effect of reducing wage levels. Don Drummond, a former chief economist at the Toronto-Dominion Bank, said in an interview about temporary foreign workers: "For sure it's depressed wage growth—with over 300,000 [foreign temporary] workers, I would use the word significantly."[4] Just how significant the impact of these foreign temporary workers has been is revealed by Unifor economist Jim Stanford, who found "over one in five net new jobs created in the entire economy from 2007 through 2012 went to one of these temporary foreign workers."[5] The resultant increase in part-time work and decrease in wages at the lower end of the income scale have been significant factors in the creation of poverty and in the widening gap between the rich and the rest of us.

The increased degree of globalization and the problems that the phenomenon creates for many working people have been facilitated by the particularly rapid technological change associated with the microelectronics revolution and the use of computers. By the mid-1970s, computers were beginning to be widely employed in industry, with soon-to-be dramatic results. Their use since then has not only

Keeping Migrant Workers' Wages Down

Even though [migrant] agricultural workers in Manitoba have the legal right to organize, they are discouraged from participating in unions. Prior to leaving Mexico, workers are advised that they will jeopardize their employment by working or relating with unions or union organizers while in Canada, and the Mexican Consulate reinforces that message upon their arrival in Canada. [According to] Manual [a Mexican migrant worker], the Mexican Consulate expressly warns workers that they should not interact with union representatives or individuals associated with unions. For this reason, some Manitoba-based workers are uneasy interacting with "outsiders," who may or may not be associated with a union.

The United Food and Commercial Workers (UFCW) Canada, one of Canada's largest private sector unions, has recorded several instances of workers being identified as union sympathizers and subsequently excluded from participating in the [migrant workers] program.

Source: Jodi Read, Sarah Zell and Lynne Fernandez, 2013, Migrant Voices: Stories of Agricultural Migrant Workers in Manitoba, *Winnipeg: Canadian Centre for Policy Alternatives-Manitoba. p. 21*

facilitated the increased globalization of economic activity, including an acceleration of the ease and rapidity by which investments can be moved around the globe, but also resulted in massive job losses in both factories and offices as a result of their use in the workplace. The loss of jobs has exerted downward pressure on wage levels at the lower end of the wage scale, and it has contributed to the growth of (generally low-paid) self-employment.

A high proportion of the jobs open to relatively unskilled school-leavers in the 1950s and 1960s—jobs that could support a family—have now disappeared. In the U.S., for example, whereas one in three Americans worked in manufacturing in the 1960s, today only one in ten holds a manufacturing job.[6] Several U.S. industrial cities—Detroit is perhaps the classic case—have been de-industrialized, hollowed out, as jobs that could once support a family have gone, leaving severely intensified poverty in place of the previously prosperous working class. This process has been memorialized by Bruce Springsteen in his song, "The Ghost of Tom Joad," referring to the classic John Steinbeck novel *The Grapes of Wrath,* which described in poignant fashion the fate of Midwestern Americans (exemplified by the Joad family in the novel) uprooted by the Great Depression of the 1930s.

A similar process has taken place in Canada, where manufacturing has declined from just under 20 percent of the economy in 1970 to about 10 percent in 2010.[7] "Since 1991, the number of manufacturing jobs has dropped by nearly 400,000, even as Canada's population has increased."[8] These jobs have relocated elsewhere or been eliminated by technology, only to be replaced by low-wage and often part-time and/or temporary work in the service sector or various forms of self-employment. The labour market has increasingly become bifurcated, with a gap between very well paid jobs and precarious jobs that are poorly paid and insecure. This shift in the structure of the labour market is an important factor in the growing gap between rich and poor in Canada.

THE ROLE OF UNIONS

So too has been the decline in the proportion of Canadian workers who are unionized. Unions produce significant tangible benefits for their members, such as higher wages, improved benefits and greater job security, for example.[9] They also bring the rule of law to the workplace. Rather than being subject to the arbitrary decisions of an owner or supervisor, unionized workers have the protection of rules and procedures that are embodied in a collective agreement that has been negotiated and agreed to by management and workers. In this respect, one can see unions, however imperfect some specific unions may be, as important factors in contributing to both a vibrant economy—adding to the total purchasing power available—and

Over the last twenty-five years, fewer and fewer Canadian workers have been represented by unions

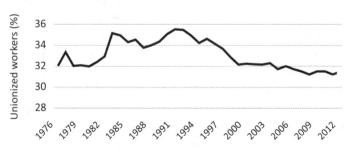

Note: Canadian data for 1996 unavilable and has therefore been interpolated.
Sources: Sharpe, Andrew, 2003, Why Are Americans More Productive than Canadians? Centre for the Study of Living Standards, CSLS Research Report 2003-03, Statistics Canada, Table 282-0078 CANSIM (database)

a more democratic society. However, the proportion of Canadian workers who enjoy the benefits of a union has been in decline in recent years, especially in the private (i.e., non-government) sector.

In the U.S., the decline in trade unionism has been worse, with the proportion of workers in the private sector who are unionized having dropped to less than 7 percent in 2013. Further, powerful right-wing interests in the U.S. are attempting to weaken unions further through the introduction at the state level of so-called right-to-work (RTW) laws, for example. Currently, about half of America's fifty states have right-to-work laws in place. These laws do *not*, as their name misleadingly suggests, give people the right to work, but rather they allow workers to opt out of paying union dues while still enjoying union benefits. They might more accurately, therefore, be thought of as "right-to-free-ride" laws. Their effect is to weaken unions and reduce wages and benefits in jurisdictions where RTW laws exist.[10] There is now a movement afoot here in Canada to introduce right-to-work legislation and related laws and policies to weaken unions further.

It is this weakening of unions that is a key factor in the rise of income inequality and the related decline of the middle class. Jordan Brennan, an economist with the Canadian union Unifor, argues that the postwar growth in union density was a major cause of the creation of a robust middle class in Canada, while the more recent trend of "de-unionization has effectively led to a redistribution of income, concentrating it back into the hands of an elite few" and eroding the middle class.[11] American economist and former secretary of labor Robert Reich argues, "The decline of labour unions in America tracks exactly the decline in the bottom 90 percent share of total earnings, a shrinkage of the middle class."[12] In Europe and North America, the growing issue is the decline of the middle class and the growing fear on the part of those still in the middle class that their economic situation will soon grow worse. Increased unionization contributed dramatically to the rise of a relatively well off "middle class" in the postwar years of economic growth; the relative decline of unions is a major factor in the erosion of the middle class and the growing inequality of the neoliberal era.

THE ECONOMIC CRISIS OF 2007–8

These problems have been accentuated by the especially dramatic economic crisis of 2007–8. For a variety of reasons, the global economy has in recent decades become increasingly "financialized"—that is, financial markets and institutions have come to play an increasingly important role in global capitalism, relative to previous times and relative also to the production of goods and services. An example of financialization has been the case of subprime mortgages, although it is important to note that subprime mortgages have been simply the most visible symptom of a deeper and more complex phenomenon. Relatively high-risk mortgages that were sold to low-income homeowners in the U.S. by banks and mortgage companies were packaged together and sold to corporate investors in the form of complex financial products—a case of the commodification (that is, turning something into a commodity, to be bought and sold for profit) of a basic human need, namely housing. Major banks and other financial institutions throughout the world purchased these financial products—these bundles of low-income homeowners' mortgages—and when the investments went sour some of the world's largest financial institutions collapsed or threatened to become bankrupt, with a powerful ripple effect throughout the global economy. Banks, and other financial and non-financial institutions, were bailed out by the U.S. government at an immense cost, measured in *trillions* of dollars, in order to prevent a slide into another Great Depression, like that of the 1930s.[13] Governments throughout the world, Canada included, pumped very large amounts of stimulus spending into their economies in order to generate a return to economic growth. The consequences of this economic crisis continue, but a complete collapse has so far been prevented by the injection into the economy of staggering sums of public money.

In Europe, however, the economic crisis of 2007–8 is far from over, and unemployment rates have reached Great Depression–era levels. In Spain and Greece, for example, official unemployment rates are above 25 percent—that is, more than one in four people are without jobs. "Unemployment is exploding across Europe," and "the 17-country euro zone is turning into an unemployment torture chamber." Youth (16–24 years of age) unemployment rates are particularly shocking: "The youth jobless rate in Spain and Greece is an astonishing 60 percent, in Italy 40 percent,"[14] and fears are being expressed about the creation of "a permanent underclass of long-term unemployed."[15] In a globalized economy, the European economic crisis has at least the potential of spilling out beyond Europe's borders

This is what a trillion dollars looks like next to a normal-sized person.

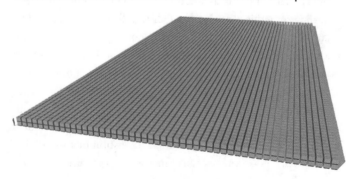

to affect other economies, including Canada's. In the meantime, the staggeringly high levels of unemployment in Europe, and especially southern Europe, are driving up poverty levels and may contribute to the expansion of long-term and very damaging complex poverty.

The result of the dramatic increase in government spending in the U.S. and, to a lesser extent, Canada to bail out a floundering capitalist economy, together with the sharp decline in tax revenues because of the economic downturn of 2007–8, has been a return to high government deficits. The legitimate fear now is that neoliberal governments will eliminate those deficits just as they eliminated the deficits of the 1980s and 1990s—by making (still more) dramatic cuts to social spending, with adverse effects on those at the bottom of the income scale. Reducing social spending of various kinds has the effect both of adding to the numbers of those living in poverty and deepening the level of poverty that they experience.

SOCIAL POLICY

The high poverty levels of the 1980s and 1990s were made worse by the dismantling of the many social policy mechanisms that had been put in place during the post-Second World War boom as a means of protecting individuals from the hazards of the inevitable ups and downs of the capitalist economy. Overall government spending — particularly government spending on social programs — was dramatically reduced during the 1980s and 1990s. For expenditures on social programs, Canada now ranks a low twenty-fourth out of the thirty Organization for Economic Cooperation and Development (OECD) nations. In addition, during the 1980s and 1990s, unemployment insurance was restructured to the disadvantage of unemployed workers and the social safety net was significantly weakened.

These and other changes in social policy were directly related to the dramatic changes in the economy. The social policy initiatives from the 1950s to the early 1970s — medicare, the Canada Assistance Plan, the Canada Pension Plan, the addition of the Guaranteed Income Supplement to Old Age Security and the reforms to unemployment insurance, for example — were funded out of the proceeds of the long postwar economic boom. Sustained economic growth and relatively low levels of unemployment generated the government revenue, the "fiscal dividend," needed to pay for new social programs. With the end of the postwar boom in the early 1970s and its replacement with a long period of relative economic stagnation, the fiscal dividend disappeared and was replaced by government deficits and the buildup of accumulated debt.

Most governments responded to the problem by cutting social spending. The various elements of the welfare state that had been erected during the postwar boom had, at least to some extent, removed the fear of unemployment and poverty that made people anxious to work at whatever wages and under whatever conditions were on offer. As early as 1975, advocates of unfettered free enterprise were express- ing concerns about the perceived consequences of the redistributive character of the welfare state in advanced capitalist economies. As the Trilateral Commission (a non-governmental body founded by U.S. billionaire David Rockefeller in 1973, comprised of corporate and other leaders from the U.S., Europe and Japan) put it, Western states had too much democracy — an "excess" of democracy — and the solution was to attack "big government."[16] If profitability was to be fully restored, the relative security created by the welfare state had to be eroded, especially because, as time went by, an increasingly competitive global economy and global labour market were making strong demands for the creation of a more "flexible" labour force.

In Canada, federal program spending as a share of gross domestic product (GDP) began to decline after 1975, when it was 20 percent of GDP. It peaked in 1982 at almost 21 percent of GDP. By 1995, even before Finance Minister Paul Martin announced massive spending cuts in that year's federal budget, government was already smaller as a share of the Canadian economy than it had been in 1975. Federal program spending in the 1996–7 fiscal year was about 13 percent of GDP, the lowest level as a share of the Canadian economy since 1950–1[17]; it continued to decline, to 12 percent of GDP for fiscal years 1999–2000 and 2000–1, and in 2011–2 it was at 14 percent, still far below the level of 1975.

The relative decline in social spending has been accompanied and facilitated by cuts in taxes, especially for higher-income Canadians and for corporations. When taxes are cut, there is less government revenue available for social spending. As Unifor economist Jim Stanford has

Government as a share of the Canadian economy has declined drastically over the past thirty-five years

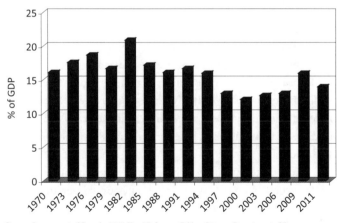

Source: Government of Canada, 2012, Fiscal Reference Tables, *Ottawa: Department of Finance*

pointed out, corporate taxes began to be cut in 1988 by the Mulroney Government, and "the combined federal-provincial statutory rate has thus declined from almost 50 percent in the early 1980s, to 29.5 percent in 2010."[18] Tax rates on high-income earners have also declined: in 1948 the top marginal income tax rate was 80 percent; in 2009 it had dropped to 43 percent.[19] In addition to being important factors in fuelling growing income inequality, such cuts reduce governments' revenue: "At the federal level alone, over $100 billion in personal and corporate tax cuts were implemented over five years, starting in 2000," and "a further $220 billion in federal tax cuts have been implemented or scheduled since 2006."[20] These are amounts of money that are *not* invested in solving poverty. On the contrary, such massive and deliberate reductions in government revenues lead to further cuts to spending and especially social spending. This is, in effect, a transfer of wealth upwards from lower-income Canadians, who rely in a multitude of ways upon government spending, to wealthier Canadians, who benefit most from these kinds of tax cuts.

Further, and on a global scale, there is evidence that staggeringly large amounts of money being transferred upwards in this way are being sheltered from taxes by being stored in offshore tax havens. A study by James S. Henry, a former chief economist at McKinsey & Company, estimates that "a significant fraction of global private financial wealth, by our estimates at least $21 to $32 trillion as of 2010, has been invested virtually tax free through the world's still expanding black hole of more than 80 offshore secrecy jurisdictions."[21]

This, too, is money not available to be invested in solving social problems such as poverty. Cuts in tax rates on corporations and wealthy individuals are justified, by those who impose them, on the grounds that they will produce increased investment, but the evidence in both Canada[22] and the U.S.[23] shows that this is not the case.

Large cuts have been made, especially in the mid-1990s, to federal programs that transfer funds to the provinces. The amount transferred to the provinces for health, post-secondary education and social assistance in 1996–7 and 1997–8 was $7 billion *less* than what would have been the case under the previous arrangements.[24] The Federal Government was "downloading" its social costs onto the provinces.

In addition, under the new Canada Health and Social Transfer (CHST), the standards that had existed under the postwar Canada Assistance Plan (CAP)—the cost-shared, federal-provincial program under which welfare and social assistance services were financed—were eliminated. Certain forms of assistance were "no longer mandated by legislation or directly supported by cost-shared transfers."[25] Previously, under CAP, in order to receive federal funds for social assistance, the provinces were required to ensure that all people judged to be in need received funding, that benefit levels met basic needs, that an appeal procedure existed, enabling people to challenge welfare decisions and that no work requirement was imposed as a condition of receiving social assistance. The removal of these standards, critics warned, would almost certainly lead to reduced levels of social assistance: the fear was expressed that the CHST "opens the way for jurisdictions to provide little or no assistance to those in need."[26]

Indeed, that is precisely what happened in the years after 1995. One by one the provinces of British Columbia, Alberta, Manitoba, Ontario, Quebec, Nova Scotia, Prince Edward Island and Newfoundland cut back their benefit rates and/or shelter allowances and altered the rules of eligibility to programs of assistance.[27] The Ontario government cut welfare rates by 21.6 percent in 1995; rates today are 55 percent lower than they were in the 1990s.[28] Several provinces introduced provincial workfare programs.

To some extent, however, this long-term dismantling of social programs was offset by the introduction of the Canada Child Tax Benefit and the National Child Benefit Supplement in 1997, paying parents a fixed amount per child and an additional amount based on income, respectively. These programs are aimed at reducing the poverty levels of families with children, and although the amounts paid to parents should be larger than they are, they nevertheless have played a role in reducing the incidence of poverty, at least as measured by the after-tax LICO, relative to what otherwise would have been the case.

This positive development notwithstanding, the social safety net has been badly damaged during the neoliberal era. For example, in a 2006 report on human rights in Canada, the United Nations Committee on Economic, Social and Cultural Rights "notes with concern that in most Provinces and Territories, social assistance benefits are lower than a decade ago, that they do not provide adequate income to meet basic needs for food, clothing and shelter, and that welfare levels are often set at less than half the Low Income Cut-Off."[29]

The trend in the U.S. has been the same. In 1996, President Bill Clinton committed to "end welfare as we know it"[30]: he replaced the Aid to Families with Dependent Children program with a new program, Temporary Assistance for Needy Families, which tightened eligibility, cut the length of time one could be on welfare and reduced benefits. The numbers of low-income Americans receiving welfare benefits have been reduced dramatically: the Urban Institute "found that one in four low-income single mothers nationwide — about 1.5 million—are jobless and without cash aid."[31]

Changes to Canada's Unemployment Insurance (UI) had the same effect. In 1989/90, the Federal Government effectively privatized UI.

As the result of Bill C-21, the government withdrew from its previous role as financial contributor to this crucial program, leaving its financing completely in the hands of employees and employers. There followed a series of changes to UI in the early to mid-1990s, each making the provision of UI more restrictive, including stricter qualifying requirements and reductions in the level and duration of benefits, for example.[32] These trends were intensified with the introduction in 1996 of Bill C-12, creating the new, renamed Employment Insurance (EI) system. The more restrictive provisions applying to EI served to accelerate the downward trend in the proportion of unemployed Canadians receiving benefits. While 74 percent of unemployed Canadians received UI benefits in 1990, only 39 percent of unemployed Canadians received EI benefits in 2001,[33] and the proportion remains roughly the same today:

Employment Insurance "Reforms" Will Weaken Rural Communities in Atlantic Canada

Rural [Prince Edward] Island communities are at risk from recent changes to Employment Insurance. Among those most concerned are members of the fishing industry who worry there won't be enough qualified people to fill seasonal positions.

Ian MacPherson, executive director of the P.E.I. Fishermen's Association, said the changes are causing concern because some valued seasonal workers may have their benefits reduced to the point where they have to move to find other work and communities are dependent on these workers.

"One of the assumptions is seasonal work is not productive work, but it is extremely productive work that has a big economic impact in the area," Mr. MacPherson said.

Source: Jesse-Ann Hennessey, 2013, "Communities Struggle Under ei Changes," PEICanada.Com, October 30

"Jobless benefits are at levels last seen in the early 1940s," some seventy years ago.[34] This erosion of EI is a process that continues. Changes in 2012 have produced, for those on EI, "lower benefits and more stringent requirements that force them to commute long distances and accept lower pay and inferior working conditions," producing what has been described as "a bad-jobs policy that rewards low-road employers by forcing job-seekers to accept low pay and bad working conditions and that will, in short order, drive down community standards."[35]

Workers of colour and Aboriginal workers are especially adversely affected by these changes to EI. Social researcher Richard Shillington observed that since the early 1990s, benefits for lower-income Canadians have been cut in half, adding, in testimony before a Senate Committee conducting hearings on poverty, housing and homelessness: "We have taken benefits from the most vulnerable for reasons that escape me."[36] The most vulnerable include those in precarious employment, and they are disproportionately workers of colour, Aboriginal workers and women.

Further, the chances of individuals successfully appealing decisions about their EI benefits have been reduced, because the federal Conservative government disbanded the Board of Referees, which previously heard EI appeals, and replaced it with the Social Security Tribunal, which will deal not only with EI appeals but also appeals with respect to the Canada Pension Plan and Old Age Security. Further, large numbers of those being appointed to the new and untested Social Security Tribunal are Conservative Party supporters: "At least half of the tribunal members, who will earn as much as $124,500 a year, have ties to the Conservatives."[37] Conservative Party appointees are most likely to be strongly influenced by neoliberal ideas and thus most opposed to social benefits for those at the bottom of the income scale.

Over the past decade and a half these changes to EI served to make employment still more precarious, with the result that wage demands have been reduced. This is no accident, since the purpose, according to Jim Stanford, is to "harmonize Canada's labour market outcomes with those of our trading partners (especially the U.S.)."[38] The goal of the reforms—"to enhance the international competitiveness of Canada's economy on a low-wage basis"—was to be achieved by "deliberately increasing the economic insecurity facing Canadian workers, hence moderating their wage demands and disciplining their behaviour in the workplace."[39] When unemployment is high and social benefits for those not employed are weak, the fear and insecurity created by the risk of job loss reduce the willingness of workers to fight for higher wages. The fear and insecurity created by higher levels of unemployment and reduced social benefits are therefore seen by the proponents and primary beneficiaries of the capitalist economy to be functional. This trend is accentuated by the gradual decline in the proportion of Canadian workers who are unionized, since the absence of a union weakens workers' bargaining power.

The current commitment to austerity measures—practised throughout North America and Europe and referring to an accentuation of neoliberal policies—has also had a deeply gendered impact. Cuts to public sector jobs disproportionately affect women, and disproportionately affect the social services that assist in the "reproduction" of families—childcare and social housing, for example. The purpose of such cuts is "to individualize and re-privatize the responsibility for caring, socially reproductive labour," and when such supports to families are cut, the burden falls most heavily on women.[40] But also, the public sector jobs by which such services are delivered are disproportionately held by women, and because public sector jobs tend to be unionized, they are relatively well-paid.

Austerity measures that cut social services hurt women in this way as well. And now seniors may be at risk: "After decades in decline, the incidence of poverty among seniors (aged 65 and older) rose 25 percent from 2007 to 2008," a shift that has disproportionately affected women and racialized seniors.[41]

The cuts in social spending and the redesign of programs were the result not only of dramatic economic changes, but also of conscious government policy. Governments have *chosen* to make certain economic and social policy changes and not to make different kinds of policy changes. With respect to unemployment, for example, political economist Ann Porter has argued that "the 1990s were marked by the severe fraying of the rights-based social safety net for most unemployed people and by the privatization or downloading of responsibility for unemployment to individuals and households."[42] More broadly, the Ontario Common Front has said, "It is not the inexorable march of global economics alone, but rather choices—choices in public budgets, and in economic and social policy" that are driving growing levels of inequality and poverty.[43]

It is in this sense that we can say, as described at the beginning of this chapter, that the incidence of poverty is related directly to the state of the economy and to the role of governments in protecting their citizens, or not, in a rapidly changing economy. Today's dominant neoliberal ideology and related government policies—that is, choices that governments have made—have dramatically reduced the role of governments in providing support to those most adversely affected by these changes. The result has been, among other things, a widening gap between the rich and the rest of us and the persistence of unacceptably large numbers of people living in poverty in Canada.

BLAMING THE POOR FOR POVERTY

Why are Canadians not outraged by these developments and by the high levels of poverty that continue to characterize this country, levels of poverty that are much higher than the Nordic countries, for example, and much higher than they need to be? Why do Canadians not demand that policies that benefit the richest Canadians be replaced by policies that produce greater equality and that reduce the still very high numbers in poverty?

A part of the reason that governments can get away with making these kinds of policy changes, even though they produce benefits for a very small proportion of the population while hurting those at the bottom of the income scale, is because of the dominance in this country of a "blame the victim" philosophy,[44] which is also an important feature of neoliberalism. Rather than explaining poverty as a function of dramatic changes in the economy and in the role of governments—as this chapter attempts to do—high levels of poverty are attributed to the personal failings of those who are poor. In many cases, the poor are demonized. When a large enough proportion of the population can be led to believe that high levels of poverty are caused by the personal failings of the poor themselves—believing they are lazy or don't take enough initiative, or they drink too much or have too many children, for example—then it becomes difficult to mount an effective opposition to the policies that make people poor. In the U.S., this trend is, if anything, even worse. A recent example is a bill introduced in Tennessee that would cut parents' social assistance if their children do not do well in school. What is the rationale for this? "If a poor child is failing, it must be the fault of low-income parents."[45] This attitude is reflected in T-shirts worn by members of the National Rifle Association that say "I hate welfare," and "If any would not work neither should he eat."[46] It is measures and attitudes such as these that have led Frances Fox Piven, long-time scholar of American poverty, to say "We've been at war for decades now... [and] it's been a war against the poor."[47]

In other cases the political right attempts simply to define poverty out of existence. The Fraser Institute, via the work of Professor Christopher Sarlo, for example, has sought to redefine poverty in a narrow, purely monetary fashion to include only those unable to afford basic physical necessities, the absence of which would jeopardize one's "long term physical well being."[48] Using this narrow and mean-spirited definition, Sarlo is driven to say, in defiance of the evidence, that "poverty, as it has been traditionally understood, has been virtually eliminated. It is simply not a major problem in Canada."[49] Some opinion leaders appear to have accepted this flawed argument. The *Winnipeg Free Press*, for example, wrote in its lead editorial of September 15, 2007, "The kind of poverty that once existed in Canada (and that can be found elsewhere in the world today) has been largely defeated." This self-satisfied attempt to define poverty out of existence is consistent with the neoliberal orientation of the

i

Federal Minister says it is not government's job to ensure children have food

In December 2013, the Harper government's Minister of Industry James Moore said, in response to a journalist's question about child poverty: "Is it my job to feed my neighbour's child? I don't think so." Reflecting the pervasive view that the poor should be left to their own devices, Moore added: "Certainly we want to make sure that kids go to school full bellied, but is that always the government's job to be there to serve people their breakfast?"

Source: <http://www.news1130.com/2013/12/15/federal-minister-says-child-poverty-not-ottawas-problem/>

Fraser Institute and much of today's corporate media, which promotes reduced government expenditures on social programs and reduced levels of taxation. And both social program spending and government revenue from taxation have been dramatically reduced in recent decades in Canada, thus magnifying the adverse effects of complex poverty.

As long as the belief is maintained that the problems of the poor are their own fault, rather than the product of economic structures and government policy choices, or that there really are no genuinely poor people in Canada at all, we are more likely to continue to vilify or ignore the poor than to mobilize to demand the changes that could dramatically reduce poverty.

COMPLEX POVERTY

Blaming the poor, an ideology that characterizes so many Canadians' understanding of why people are poor, is accentuated in the case of complex poverty. Complex poverty tends to be deep and long lasting and is often psychologically debilitating. Those who experience complex poverty suffer not just a shortage of income, as debilitating as that alone can be in a monetized society, but also a host of other causally inter-related consequences such as inadequate housing, low levels of educational attainment, poor health, racism of various kinds in many cases, a relatively high incidence of violence via street gang activity and the illegal drug trade, and perhaps most importantly, high levels of unemployment and low levels of labour force participation. These factors feed on each other and create a deep and often intractable form of poverty. The roots of this complex poverty—which in many cases is spatially concentrated and racialized—are to be found in the dramatic socio-economic changes of the past thirty to forty years, as described in the last chapter. Nevertheless, it is those people, families and communities experiencing this complex form of poverty who are particularly prone to being blamed for their circumstances.

How we understand and explain poverty has important

implications for how, or even if, we set out to solve it. The blaming the victim mode of explanation is especially problematic because of the policy implications that follow from it. That is why it is especially important to understand that however much it may *appear* that those living in complex poverty are the cause of their own problems, and however much it may be the case that at times their behaviour reinforces that appearance, the root causes of complex poverty are socio-economic. Change the socio-economic circumstances, and the vast majority of those living in complex poverty will change their behaviour. To blame the poor for their poverty, as so often happens, is to fail to see beneath the surface appearance of things.

Blaming the victims of poverty has a long history, going back at least to the Poor Laws and workhouses of the British Elizabethan era. In the U.S., the distinction has long been made between the "deserving" and "undeserving" poor: some of the poor are undeserving because their behaviour — often characterized as immoral or otherwise negative — is thought to make them the authors of their own misfortune. In the 1960s, this more "cultural" form of explanation — the view that the cause of poverty is the cultural attributes of those who are poor, rather than more structural factors like changes in the character of labour markets or in the role of governments — took deep root, especially in the U.S. in the work of Oscar Lewis (1961; 1969) and Daniel Patrick Moynihan (1965).

Lewis argued that the poor, by which he meant those living in complex poverty, have cultural/psychological characteristics that lock them into a life of poverty at an early age and this becomes "a way of life that is passed down from generation to generation along family lines."[1] Even if opportunities arise, Lewis argued, the poor cannot take advantage because they are locked into dysfunctional cultural and behavioural patterns that prevent their doing so: they adapt to their poverty and accept it as a given, have feelings of helplessness and dependency and are unable to defer gratification, for example. This cultural form of explanation leads to the conclusion that the poor are undeserving: they are poor because of the way they behave; they choose to behave in these ways; and therefore they are undeserving of sympathy or support. This conclusion has obvious policy implications that turn out to be consistent with the neoliberalism of the past thirty years: there is little point in attempting to solve poverty.

Moynihan made a similar argument in his influential and controversial study *The Negro Family: The Case for National Action*, in which he famously found the source of the problem to be "the deterioration of the Negro family," as evidenced by its matriarchal structure. In female-headed families in Black ghettoes, he argued, children, especially male children, were not properly socialized, resulting in a "tangled web of pathology" (they are "lazy"; "criminal and disorderly"; "immoral"). A careful reading of both Lewis and Moynihan finds the roots of their arguments in structural phenomena, in particular an absence of paid employment. But this structural side of their argument was lost in the easier forms of explanation that they highlighted, in which the cause of poverty was the poor themselves. And when the poor are to blame, the solution is to change the poor, not the system.

Oscar Lewis on the culture of poverty

"The people in the culture of poverty have a strong feeling of marginality, of helplessness, of dependency, of not belonging.... Along with this feeling of powerlessness is a widespread feeling of inferiority, or personal unworthiness."

Source: Oscar Lewis, 1998, "The Culture of Poverty," Society 35, 2

The argument that the poor are the authors of their own grief and are not deserving of our (governmental) assistance is not only consistent with neoliberal ideology, but is also — despite its inadequacy — an apparently obvious and therefore easy explanation. It focuses on surface phenomena, the behaviour and cultural attributes of the poor, and obscures the deeper structural phenomena, especially the dramatically changed character of the labour market and the neoliberal-inspired withdrawal of the state from support for the poor.

Furthermore, those who benefit from the system as it now exists do not want to change it. To promote their own interests, they support particular interpretations of events and phenomena. As Paul Watt, a British professor of urban studies has argued: "Politics is an arena in which different interest groups seek to establish a particular narrative or version of events as a means to pursue political objectives."[2] If the poor are the cause of their own poverty, then no systemic change is needed. Indeed, as Charles Murray, an American researcher who influenced U.S. President Ronald Reagan, argued, social welfare programs only worsen matters, a conclusion consistent with the emergent neoliberalism of the Reagan years, which sought to "get governments off the backs of the people"[3] and to do so by cutting social spending.

Further, the poor are not typically the authors of the narratives by which their circumstances are described. They do not produce the images and metaphors by which they are depicted. They do not control how they are publicly represented. Those who do are not only those with more power and an interest in maintaining that power, but also those who typically have no direct knowledge of the poor and their lives. From the outside, and with differing interests, they construct a narrative that situates the poor relative to a white, middle-class and suburban way of life taken to be the norm. The urban poor are not part of this norm. They are the "Other." The explanation for their difference must therefore be that they have individual or ethno-racial deficiencies. Their lives, their neighbourhoods, are a "tangled web of pathology." They are lazy, criminal, disorderly, immoral; they become the "undeserving poor."

Those geographic areas inhabited by the poor are similarly seen as dark and immoral, occupied by strangers, and their depiction often takes on a racialized character. African-American anthropologist Elijah Anderson observes:

> White newcomers in particular continue to view the ghetto as a mysterious and unfathomable place that breeds drugs, crime, prostitution, unwed mothers, ignorance and mental illness. It symbolizes persistent poverty and imminent danger, personified in the young black men who walk the [ghetto] streets.[4]

These are "discourses of demonization."[5] We demonize, and thus blame, the poor, and especially the racialized poor. Katz describes this as "the peculiar American tendency to transform poverty from a product of politics and economics into a matter of individual behaviour."[6] Such a transformation illustrates prominent U.S. sociologist C. Wright Mills's important distinction between those matters that are truly "individual" or "private" troubles, and those that are "public issues."[7] Spatially concentrated racialized poverty is a public issue, with identifiable causes rooted in a rapidly changing global political economy, but it is often depicted as an individual or private problem, caused by the behaviour of the poor themselves.

However, another stream of thought, long present in the study of urban poverty in the U.S., re-emerged in the mid-1980s, primarily in the work of prominent University of Chicago sociologist William Julius Wilson.

POVERTY AND SOCIO-ECONOMIC STRUCTURE

In *The Truly Disadvantaged*, Wilson described the circumstances of the new, complex urban poverty in American inner cities and laid out the basis of a more structural explanation. He did not, quite appropriately, abandon the insights of the behavioural/cultural forms of explanation. But he argued that these behavioural/cultural manifestations of the new urban poverty were responses, and/or adaptations, to the new material conditions that had emerged in inner cities. Change these material conditions, he argued, and the behaviour and culture will change, albeit gradually.[8]

Wilson argued that the root cause of the new urban poverty was the changing character of the labour market. The industrial/manufacturing jobs that those with modest levels of education could previously have relied upon to achieve a standard of living that could support a family were leaving U.S. urban centres for the suburbs, the Sunbelt and beyond U.S. borders. These were the jobs taken up earlier in the century by the waves of African-Americans who migrated from the U.S. South to northern cities in search of better lives.[9] Over the past four decades, very large numbers of these manufacturing jobs have been replaced by precarious jobs — service sector, part-time, low-wage, no benefits, no security, no union — with which it was especially difficult to support a family. The consequence, Wilson argued, was that large numbers of inner-city residents, especially African-Americans, were without work, and the widespread absence of work produced changes to family structures and a variety of behavioural adaptations, many of them negative.

African-American scholars had long identified the importance of the labour market, and of racism, in U.S. urban poverty. W.E.B. DuBois found that although African-Americans had a higher labour force participation rate than whites in Philadelphia, they worked in lower-paid jobs, and he identified their segregation, social exclusion and relative family instability — themes resurrected in the last part of the twentieth century — as products of a variety of factors, chief amongst which was racism: the "widespread feeling all over the land … that the Negro is something less than an American."[10] Even at that early date, DuBois identified the behaviourial characteristics of the Black lower class that would in the 1960s be seized upon by the "culture of poverty" and "tangled web of pathology" interpretations;

Source: Steve Sacks, 2013, "The Walmart Woes," Nov. 20. <http://www.cagle.com/2013/11/walmart-woes/>. Reprinted with permission from Cagle Cartoons

the difference was that DuBois firmly situated these phenomena in material circumstances, including racism. Later in the century, other African-American scholars — Charles Johnson,[11] E. Franklin Frazier, St. Clair Drake and Horace Cayton and Oliver Cromwell Cox, for example — emphasized racism and its deep and lasting effects as being central in explaining the relatively high levels of poverty and social exclusion experienced by African-Americans. In *The Truly Disadvantaged,* Wilson developed this argument further, emphasizing that growing numbers of African-Americans were trapped in inner cities hollowed out by deindustrialization and suburbanization and that the effects of racism were less the result of currently existing restrictions than of the weight of a racist history, which, when combined with the loss of jobs, became internalized and manifested itself in the behaviourial/cultural forms identified by Lewis and Moynihan. But it was the absence of paid employment, Wilson insisted, that created the "underclass" and the various forms of poverty-related behaviour now identified with complex poverty.

The post-1960s flight of manufacturing jobs from U.S. inner cities, together with the suburbanization of those who could afford to leave,[12] led to inner cities being "hollowed out," worsening the situations of those, disproportionately African-Americans, left behind. Whole neighbourhoods came to be characterized by the relative absence of residents in the labour market, which in turn made it difficult for young people to learn the cultural norms associated with work or to find work by means of connections with family members or neighbours who have jobs, which is the traditional way for young people to get their first job.[13] The result was a Black youth employment crisis.[14] With fewer and fewer people working in the inner cities, women, Wilson argued, increasingly chose to raise children on their own. What was the point in having an unemployed male in the home?

The result was a dramatic increase in the numbers and proportions of inner-city households that were single-parent, female-headed families — what Moynihan had identified as the cause of inner-city problems. Even though he did identify their ultimate roots in labour market changes, Moynihan placed the weight of causality on "the deterioration of the Negro family." Wilson, by contrast, placed the weight of the explanation in the dramatic, post-1960s changes in the structure of the labour market that have been the consequences of globalization, deindustrialization and the rise of neoliberalism.

Loic Wacquant, French sociologist of urban marginality, develops a similar structural explanation for complex poverty in urban centres: "the double retrenchment of the labour market and the welfare state from the urban core." But he places the greatest emphasis on the neoliberal abandonment of the welfare state:

> In the final analysis, however, it is the *collapse of public institutions*, resulting from state policies of urban abandonment and leading to the punitive containment of the black sub-proletariat [as seen in the astonishingly high rates of imprisonment of young Black men in the U.S., and Aboriginal men in Canada] that emerges as the most distinct cause of entrenched marginality in the American metropolis.[15]

Sudhir Venkatesh, an American urban sociologist, similarly describes the virtual abandonment since the 1970s, by all levels of government, of the Robert Taylor Homes, the vast stretch of public housing projects on Chicago's south side that became the poster child for the American version of spatially concentrated racialized (i.e., complex) poverty.

Wilson's work has also laid the foundation for a deeper understanding of street gangs and the related growth of the illegal drug trade and violence, which have been such a central feature of the new urban poverty over the past three decades in particular. John Hagedorn, a leading authority on street gangs, for example, has argued that this is a global phenomenon,[16] a product of the global economic change that has produced what American author Mike Davis has described as "urbanization ... radically decoupled from industrialization" — vast numbers of people leaving the land and relocating to cities where there are no jobs for them — resulting in "the mass production of slums," the creation, indeed, of *A Planet of Slums.*[17]

For the first time in human history, half of the world's population now lives in urban centres.[18] But unlike the industrial revolution of the nineteenth century, when English peasants were forced off the land and into the "dark satanic mills" of a rapidly industrializing England, the horrifying conditions of which were described by Friedrich Engels and countless others, today people throughout the world are moving off the land and into urban centres where they do not work in dark satanic mills. There is no, or almost no, wage labour. The conditions that result are horrendous. And out of these circumstances, these material conditions, particular forms of behaviour and cultural adaptations emerge, including the rise of street gangs, with young men struggling to find a way to make a living in an increasingly jobless but networked world saturated with globalized invitations to enjoy the benefits of the consumer lifestyle. The same structural explanation — along with the effects of colonialism — has recently been used to explain the emergence, especially in western Canada, of Aboriginal street gangs.[19]

Adverse material circumstances produce behaviourial and cultural responses. It is essential to see beneath the behaviourial symptoms to find the material causes. It is not, however, that inner-city residents, faced with the very difficult material circumstances of inner-city life, simply acquiesce. They are resilient and creative; they resist.[20] A strong sense of community exists in many inner-city neighbourhoods, and many strengths are to be found there.

Lewis and Moynihan and many others were not wrong in identifying culture and behaviour as an important part of the problem. But they were wrong in seeing it as the root cause and as being unchangeable. Change the material conditions, and the behaviour will change too, although neither will change instantly. This understanding is important, indeed essential, if we are to be successful in solving the inter-related problems of complex poverty.

COMPLEX POVERTY IN CANADA

Understanding and explaining poverty in Canada has long been plagued by the same individualistic, blame-the-poor mode of explanation that has been so powerful in the U.S. This was the case in Winnipeg's pre-Second World War North End, for example, where Eastern European immigrants who spoke "odd" languages, dressed differently and ate "smelly" food were called "bohunks", "polacks", "dumb hunkies" and "drunkards" and were subjected to many forms of discrimination and socio-economic exclusion.[21] Their depiction — by those who rarely, if ever, ventured into the North End — justified the lack of public investment there that has long characterized Winnipeg's political economy.[22] A "poor-bashing" discourse has continued in Canada.

Studies of poverty in Canada were rare after the first decades of the century, but the late 1960s and early 1970s saw a surge of interest. This was likely attributable to the radicalism of the 1960s, the sense of optimism about the possibilities for social change and events in the U.S., including the mid-1960s War on Poverty — the major attempt to eradicate U.S. poverty that was undermined by the soaring costs of the war in Vietnam — and the 1962 publication of Michael Harrington's influential study of what was then a largely hidden poverty, *The Other America*. The Economic Council of Canada and the Canadian Senate produced studies of poverty that said rather dramatic things by today's standards. The Economic Council called the high levels of poverty in Canada at that time a "disgrace." The Senate Report called poverty "our national shame," said that the social welfare system had "outlived its usefulness," called for a guaranteed annual income and said that "the system has failed because it has treated the symptoms of poverty and left the disease itself untouched."[23] A more radical alternative to the Senate study, called *The Real Poverty Report*, was published on the grounds that the Senate Report did not adequately address the systemic causes of the "actual production of poverty."[24] Still, in discussions of poverty of the time, reference was only occasionally made to Aboriginal people and the effects of colonization,[25] and little was said about immigration because the 1967 changes to immigration laws that would result in the dramatic growth in the numbers of "visible minorities" in large urban centres was just underway. Thus the racialization of poverty in urban centres was not at all a focus in Canada at that time, as it was in the U.S.

What was said frequently in the late 1960s and early 1970s was that the poverty of the time was a "new poverty," different from what had existed during the Great Depression of the 1930s, when poverty was the norm because the majority of working-class people were poor. By the 1960s, by contrast, the vast majority of Canadians were seen to be doing relatively well, and the poor were thought to be residual categories of people left out of the benefits of the postwar boom: the aged; those in certain regions, Atlantic Canada for example; the then relatively few female-headed families; and Aboriginal people living on rural and northern reserves. Occasionally mention was made of African-Canadians, particularly in Nova Scotia.[26] There was very little about spatially concentrated urban poverty, with the partial exception of Montreal and to a lesser extent Toronto,[27] although in some cases[28] the characteristics of the urban poor that are today more widely known — a high proportion of female-headed families, high rates of unemployment, for example — were identified. It was only in the mid-1980s and especially the 1990s that the image of urban poverty as spatially concentrated and racialized — i.e., complex poverty — began to emerge.

This new form of poverty emerged partly in response to new immigration patterns, which changed dramatically following reforms to Canadian immigration law in 1967, with a tripling of the number of visible minority immigrants in Canada between 1981 and 2001. This was especially the case in Canada's largest urban centres: the visible minority population increased from 13.6 percent of Toronto's population in 1981 to 36.8 percent in 2001; in Vancouver it was 13.9 percent and 36.9 percent.[29] In some cities, there was spatial concentration but relatively little racialization of poverty.[30] Hajnal found that "on one hand race greatly influences one's chances of living in concentrated urban poverty. On the other hand, most people in concentrated urban poverty are in fact white."[31] Others found a high incidence of both spatially concentrated and racialized poverty in Canadian cities. Fong and Shibuya, for example, said:

> We found that residents of areas with such high levels of spatial separation of the poor were mostly members of visible minorities: more than 40 % of Asians and blacks in

Montreal, and nearly 40% of blacks in Halifax, lived in areas with poverty rates above 30% ... in Canada, the spatial separation of the poor from the general non-poor population is confined largely to visible minorities (blacks and Asians).[32]

More recently, the United Way of Greater Toronto found not only that poverty had significantly increased in Toronto between 1981 and 2001, and increased further in 2005, but also that it had taken on a spatially concentrated and racialized character. Urban geographer David Hulchanski found the same for the period 1970–2000: "The proportion of low- and very low-income neighbourhoods increased from 19% to 50%, and the proportion of high- and very high-income neighbourhoods increased from 15% to 18%," while the numbers of middle-income people declined.[33] Hulchanski also found that the geographic location of low-income neighbourhoods shifted outwards, from the inner city to the suburbs, and that not only was poverty growing, but also it was increasingly racialized. The same pattern has been found in Vancouver over the period 1970 to 2005.[34] Income gains have been made disproportionately in neighbourhoods that are white and native-born, while the neighbourhoods that have experienced the greatest income declines are increasingly located in the suburbs and are predominately populated by foreign-born visible minorities. Poverty in Winnipeg has been found to be high and racialized, but, unlike Toronto, Vancouver and, to a lesser extent, Montreal, it is disproportionately concentrated in the inner city, with Aboriginal people disproportionately among the poor.[35] It is now the case that in Canada, as in the U.S., poverty is all too frequently a racialized phenomenon

Although the incidence of spatially concentrated racialized poverty is not as high in Canada as in the U.S., and although it varies considerably by city, the phenomenon does exist, often in association with the presence of public housing,[36] and as is the case in the U.S., racialized poverty produces behaviourial/cultural responses typically associated with complex poverty:

> The spatial concentration of poverty is not merely about the geographical distribution of a group of people in urban space. It can also lead to social and psychological processes with far-reaching consequences for the living conditions of the poor.[37]

Political scientist Grace-Edward Galabuzi emphasizes "the growing social exclusion of racialized group members" and identifies its increasing spatial concentration in urban centres.[38] Again, these phenomena are rooted solidly in material changes:

> Globalization-generated pressures have led to the retreat by the state from its social obligations, leading to social deficits that impact racialized communities disproportionately.... Young immigrants face a crisis of unemployment, despair, and violence. They are disproportionately targets of contact with the criminal justice system.[39]

THE CHARACTERISTICS OF COMPLEX POVERTY

The defining feature of complex poverty is that it is characterized by a host of causally inter-related factors beyond, but of course directly related to, a shortage of money. These include bad housing, low educational outcomes and poor health, the adverse effects of racism and colonialism, a higher than average level of neighbourhood-based street gang activity and associated violence, high levels of unemployment and detachment from the labour force, social exclusion and powerful psychological effects that are the result of peoples' internalizing the complex poverty-related problems with which they must contend. David Butler-Jones, Canada's Chief Public Health Officer, has called these "a cluster of disadvantages of which economic poverty is a key driver."[40] These multiple aspects of complex poverty feed on each other, in an inter-connected and cumulative fashion, producing a downward cycle in many peoples' lives and a sense that they are caught in a web from which they cannot escape.

Housing

Inadequate housing, for example, is typically a factor in the lives of those living in complex poverty. There is a shortage of low-income rental housing all across Canada that has reached crisis proportions.[41] People who are poor are living in housing that is over-crowded, in need of repairs and more expensive than they can afford. It is often poorly insulated, thus driving up heating bills and worsening their shortage of income. Mould and bedbugs are common problems,[42] and along with overcrowding these factors can lead to health problems. David Butler-Jones has said that "inadequate housing can result in numerous negative health outcomes, ranging from respiratory disease and asthma due to molds and poor ventilation, to mental health impacts associated with overcrowding."[43] Poor housing and related health problems can, in turn, adversely affect children's chances of success at school.

Slum landlords frequently make matters worse by refusing to make repairs or even to spend on basic maintenance and squeezing as many tenants as they can into the buildings they own. One strategy that low-income tenants adopt is to move frequently, constantly in search of slightly more decent housing.[44] But frequent moves make schooling more problematic for children. As long as two decades ago the problem of frequent moves for children was reported in Winnipeg:

Migrancy (frequent movers) is a particular problem for inner city children …. In a 1992 review of inner city schools, the lowest migrancy rate (proportion of children moving per year in the school population) was 40.6 percent. The highest rate was 84.7 percent…. Some children have been in 13 schools by 11 years of age…. In a nine-month period in 1992/93, there were 3,058 single-parent moves out of a possible 3,553.[45]

Homelessness, too, is now all too common in Canada. As economist Lars Osberg put it:

Part of the "new normal" of Canadian urban life is daily observation of beggars at major intersections, homeless people on sidewalks and street people collecting bottles. I am old enough to remember that they were not always there.[46]

And as Stephen Gaetz, who has written extensively on homelessness observes, this too is a function of neoliberalism and the withdrawal of the Federal Government in the early 1990s from the funding of social housing, which then "undermined important infrastructure that plays a major role in the prevention of homelessness, and in helping people move out of homelessness."[47]

In a 1998 report, the United Nations' Committee on Economic, Social and Cultural Rights said, "The Committee is gravely concerned that such a wealthy country as Canada has allowed the problem of homelessness and inadequate housing to grow to such proportions

Social Housing in Canada
Annual social housing production under NHA Section 95,
compared to all dwelling starts (1979-2011)

All values approximate.

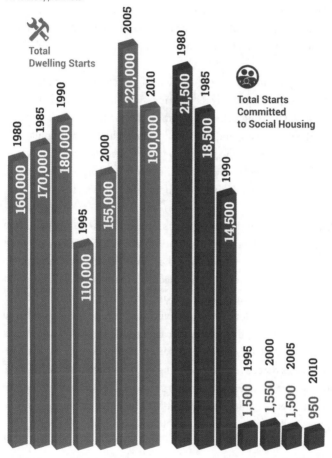

Total Dwelling Starts

1980: 160,000
1985: 170,000
1990: 180,000
1995: 110,000
2000: 155,000
2005: 220,000
2010: 190,000

Total Starts Committed to Social Housing

1980: 21,500
1985: 18,500
1990: 14,500
1995: 1,500
2000: 1,550
2005: 1,500
2010: 950

that the mayors of Canada's ten largest cities have now declared homelessness a national disaster." A recent study of homelessness in Canada by Steven Gaetz estimated that "at least 200,000 Canadians access homeless emergency services or sleep outside in a given year," and he roots this problem in the low-income housing crisis, in turn a product of the neoliberal withdrawal of the state:

> We do know that the homelessness crisis was created through dramatically reduced investments in affordable and social housing in the 1990s, shifts in income supports and the declining spending power of almost half of the population since that time. Currently many Canadians are at risk of homelessness because of the high cost (and unavailability) of housing, inadequate incomes and family violence.[48]

The root cause of the housing crisis for low-income people is that approximately 95 percent of new housing is built by private, for-profit contractors and developers, and they produce what is most likely to make a profit, not what is most needed. There is little, if any, profit to be made in producing rental housing for very low-income people, so for-profit developers do not build such housing. Because social assistance rates and wages in precarious jobs are so low in Canada today, those reliant upon such income cannot afford to pay the high rental rates that cover the costs of newly constructed rental housing. So low-income housing does not get built, at least in anything like the numbers of units needed. If it is to be built, governments have to be involved. But in 1993, consistent with neoliberal ideology, the Federal Government got out of the funding of social housing — that is, housing that is subsidized — with the result that we have an enormous shortage of low-income rental housing right across the country.

Adequate and affordable housing serves as the necessary foundation for peoples' efforts to extricate themselves from poverty because without a home, poor peoples' health is likely to worsen, jobs are harder to secure, children's schooling is adversely affected, and so on. The shortage of such housing for low-income people contributes to the perpetuation of poverty, and especially complex poverty.

Health

Complex poverty also includes poor health. There is now so much evidence linking complex poverty to poor health that it is almost a truism: "The health of people with lower incomes is invariably worse than that of people with higher incomes, regardless of the health measure used."[49] It is the socio-economic conditions in which people live that are the most important determinants of their health. In Saskatoon's low-income West End and in Winnipeg's North End, to take just two examples, the incidence of every conceivable health problem — heart and circulatory disease, all forms of cancer, liver and kidney disease, stress-related health problems, infant mortality, incidence of hospitalization, accidents — is higher than in the rest of those cities.[50] Poor health is both a part of, and is caused by, the prevalence of complex poverty in these neighbourhoods.

The higher incidence of poverty amongst Aboriginal peoples is a causal factor in their relatively poor health outcomes.[51] United Nations studies have found that "life expectancy for Aboriginal peoples is seventeen years less than for non-Aboriginal peoples; rate(s) of tuberculosis for First Nations people was 35 times higher than for the non-Aboriginal population."[52] Aboriginal scholar Michael Hart observes: "Numerous studies over the decades have identified the serious problems with housing and infrastructure for Indigenous peoples such as overcrowding, safety associated with water quality, and an accumulation of [housing] units in need of major repair."[53] Hence, their poor health. He points out that while Aboriginal people generally fare more poorly than Canadians in virtually every aspect of health, the differences virtually disappear when studies control for socio-economic conditions. "In other words, 'Aboriginality' is not the significant factor; the social determinants of health are." Complex and racialized poverty makes people sick; being sick in turn increases the likelihood of being poor.

In some cases, poor health is attributable to the inadequate diets that many of the poor must endure. Generally, the cost of food in Canada has risen 63 percent since 1995,[54] while real incomes have stagnated. It is even worse for those who live in northern communities. Linda Gionet and Shirin Roshanafshar found that food costs in most isolated northern communities are, on average, about double the costs in southern Canada.[55] Lynne Fernandez and Nadine Tonn found that in northern Manitoba communities 75 percent of households suffered moderate or severe levels of food insecurity, more than eight times the incidence of food insecurity in Canada as a whole.[56] Similar problems prevail in low-income urban neighbourhoods. Supermarkets have moved out of low-income neighbourhoods, following the money to the better-off suburbs, with the result that low-income areas become "food deserts."[57] Poor people — large numbers of whom do not own cars — are thus forced to shop for food at small corner grocery stores where prices are much higher and the variety and quality of foods much lower.

Even worse, large numbers of Canadians now rely on food banks. It is scandalous that in a country as economically strong as Canada so many people — 833,098 in March 2013, 36 percent of whom were children and youth, although children and youth comprise just 21 percent of Canada's population[58] — should have to rely on food banks, which emerged, as did increased homelessness, in the early 1980s as a product of the emergence of neoliberalism. Food banks typically offer food that is of relatively poor quality. The use of food banks is directly related to the low-income housing crisis — rents are now so high in relation to social assistance rates and wages in precarious jobs that many poor people have little if anything left for food after paying their rent and are thus forced to turn to food banks to eat. This is yet another example of how the elements of complex poverty interact with each other to make the lives of poor people still more difficult.

Education

Poverty, and especially complex poverty, is also causally interconnected with poor educational outcomes. As long-time Canadian educational researchers Jane Gaskell and Ben Levin describe it: "Socio-economic status (SES) is the single most powerful factor associated with educational and other life outcomes, as has been found in virtually every important study of these issues, over time, in every country where such studies have been conducted."[59] And poor

Poverty and education feed on each other, creating a vicious cycle

Poverty

Poor educational outcomes

educational outcomes lead to more poverty. The universal pattern is this: the higher the level of poverty, the lower the level of educational attainment; low levels of educational attainment, in turn, increase the likelihood of poverty. Low levels of educational attainment also increase the likelihood of incarceration: "A number of studies have found that school performance in adolescence is among the strongest predictors of whether a person will get in trouble with the law, whether as a youth or adult."[60] In some low-income neighbourhoods in Winnipeg's North End, for example, 20 percent of young people graduate high school on time, while more than 90 percent of young people in suburban Winnipeg graduate on time.[61] We see the same pattern for Aboriginal people in Canada: a particularly high incidence of poverty, relatively low literacy skills, low early development instrument scores (i.e., low levels of readiness for kindergarten at age five) and low educational outcomes, which in turn create "a gap in Aboriginal employment between the highly literate and the poorly literate of almost thirty percentage points."[62] Those who do not have grade 12 are less likely to find a good job and thus more likely to be poor in the future. A vicious cycle is set in motion.

Poor educational outcomes lead to low levels of employment and/ or entrapment in precarious jobs that do not pay enough and are not secure enough to support a family. William Julius Wilson has argued that the high incidence of single-parent, female-headed Black families in the U.S. — a high proportion of whom experience poverty — is a direct consequence of the low levels of employment of Black men in low-income urban centres.[63] This, together with the high rates of incarceration of Black men, produces "a long-term decline in the proportion of black men, and particularly young black men, who are in a position to support a family."[64] According to American professors Kathryn Edin and Maria Kefalas, young, poor women choose to have children anyway because the "opportunity costs" of their doing so are so low — unlike middle-class women, poor women are not giving up potentially satisfying career opportunities by having a baby at an early age. On the contrary, they see no attractive career opportunities for themselves, and "thus, for the poor, childbearing often rises to the top of the list of potential meaning-making activities from mere lack of competition."[65] Thus a lack of success in the labour market — itself a function of, among other factors, low levels of education, which are a product of poverty — is an important factor in the changing character of the family structures of those who experience racialized poverty. The relatively high levels of street-level violence associated with street gang activity and the illegal drug trade is a direct consequence of the poor employment prospects of young men experiencing racialized poverty.[66] In neighbourhoods and communities where relatively few people are employed, the unemployment problem reproduces itself. Young people do not learn the cultural norms associated with paid employment and do not have family and friends who can connect them with a first job, so they too disproportionately experience inadequate employment or no employment. As in so many cases, this is a factor in producing the vicious cycle by which poverty is reproduced across generations.

Social Exclusion

Poverty also increases the likelihood of social exclusion — people who are poor are less likely to be able to participate fully in what mainstream society has to offer. They may become marginalized from important aspects of the dominant culture. Their children, for example, are less likely to have the opportunity to learn music or dance, or to play organized sports, with all the benefits these activities produce for children. Adults are less likely to be able to attend concerts or folk festivals, or take vacations away from home, or even go to a public library. It may be surprising to many Canadians to learn the extent to which those who are poor can be excluded from much of what the rest of us take for granted. For example, a 46-year-old grandmother attending an adult literacy program in Lord Selkirk Park, a large public housing project in Winnipeg's low-income North End, described being excited about a class trip to the library: "I even got a library card which I had never had before."[67] In many large public housing projects residents are often burdened with the stigma and stereotypes associated with their complex and racialized poverty, as a consequence of which many are fearful of moving beyond the borders of their housing complex.[68] The same is the case in many rural and northern Aboriginal communities. Referring to Pikangikum, an

Joe's story: Being poor means having no choices

"When you are poor you have no choices. I hate having no choices and having to be forced to beg on the streets. Having choices gives you self-respect, dignity, self-esteem, self-control and confidence. But this is lost when you are forced to use food banks and line up at a soup kitchen every day.... I hate it when my dignity is undermined and my self-respect swallowed in exchange for a meal somewhere.... But it isn't really hate that I feel. I am hurt. Very deeply hurt. That people like me, that people who are poor, are ill treated — verbally and mentally mistreated and forced to live in such terrible conditions because people do not see us as deserving of more."

— Joe is a homeless resident with mental health issues in inner-city Winnipeg.

Source: CCPA-MB, 2009, "I Just Want to Have a Decent Home: Joe's Story," Fast Facts, July 8

Ojibwa community in northwestern Ontario, the band manager said that the community sees itself as "its own little world," and added that the idea of leaving "is scary."[69] They are spatially, as well as socially and economically, excluded.

Social exclusion, together with the effects of racism and colonialism, also leads people who experience complex poverty to have negative interactions with and interpretations of various arms of government. This increases their social exclusion.

Children's aid societies, for example, are often feared by the poor because so many of their children are taken away by these agencies. In the case of Manitoba, there are approximately 10,000 children "in care." More than 80 percent of them are Aboriginal.[70] This is directly related to poverty. Cindy Blackstock, Executive Director of First Nations Child and Family Caring Society of Canada, is reported to have said that "study after study shows the single best indicator of child welfare is income level, and as long as Aboriginal kids are the poorest in Canada, they're going to end up in care more often."[71] Jon Gerrard , a former leader of Manitoba's Liberal Party, wrote: "A child living in a low-income area is 47 times more likely to be taken into care than one living in a high-income area. Alarmingly, one in seven children in Manitoba's low-income areas has been in the care of Child and Family Services."[72] It is no surprise, therefore, that Aboriginal families fear child welfare agencies. Gerrard adds: "During the time I practiced as a pediatrician at the Children's Hospital in Winnipeg, I was shocked to meet people who were very fearful of contact with Manitoba's Child and Family Services system."

People living in complex poverty often have similarly negative attitudes about other "systems," as they call them. This is the case for the educational system because so many who are poor, and especially the racialized poor, have had negative experiences with school. Education scholar Yatta Kanu describes "the privileging and normalization of dominant values and beliefs in the public school system, [and] the exclusion of Aboriginal and other ethnic minority values."[73] Bernard Schissel and Terry Wotherspoon, professors who have studied Aboriginal education in Canada, add that "numerous studies and reports in recent years have drawn attention to the dark side of education, implicating schools in processes that have badly damaged or even destroyed the lives and futures of many Aboriginal people and their communities."[74] This is a major part of the reason that so many low-income Aboriginal people distrust and even fear schools, thus aggravating their social exclusion.

The Criminal Justice System

The same is the case with the police and the criminal justice system, and again it is because poor peoples' interactions with these systems are so often negative. Racialized policing is a reality across Canada, affecting those who are the racialized poor; it is wildly disproportionately the case that provincial and federal prisons in western Canada, for example, are occupied by people of Aboriginal descent and that violence against Aboriginal women — domestic abuse, murder and police violence, for example — is much higher than for the population at large.[75] Sharene Razack and Lisa Priest have provided chilling accounts of the racist-inspired murders of Pamela George in Regina and Helen Betty Osborne in The Pas, both Aboriginal women, and the failure of police forces to respond as they ought to have done.[76] Indeed, Amnesty International reported that "despite assurances to the contrary, police in Canada have often failed to provide Indigenous women with an adequate standard of protection."[77] Elizabeth Comack provides numerous examples of "starlight tours," where police take Aboriginal people to the outskirts of a city and leaving them there to their own devices, sometimes leading to their deaths.[78] As a result, it should come as no surprise that Aboriginal people are suspicious of, and in many cases fearful of, the RCMP and other police services. Human Rights Watch links violence against Indigenous women directly to inequality, poverty and colonialism, which is consistent with the notion of the inter-related impacts of complex poverty.[79]

In low-income neighbourhoods, the incidence of crimes against persons and property is typically higher than it is elsewhere in the city. Street gang activity, the illegal drug trade and associated violence tend to be concentrated in very low-income neighbourhoods.[80] Many residents of such neighbourhoods — mothers and grandmothers especially — fear for their safety and fear that their children may become caught up in such violent and illegal activity. In some cases, mothers do not let their youngsters out after dark, for fear of violence.[81] This is the case in the U.S. as well. In Chicago, 506 homicides were reported in 2012 alone. The vast majority of these occurred in the city's low-income south and west sides, leading many mothers there to keep their children inside from the time school ends, and one mother, typical of many others, to say, "I don't go out at night."[82] The resulting high levels of stress are causal factors in various health problems; children may fear being harassed on the way to, from or at school, adversely affecting their chances of success at school. People living in these low-income neighbourhoods, in turn, are more likely to experience various adverse forms of policing[83] and are more likely to be incarcerated at some time in their lives in a provincial or federal penal institution.

Racism

These various factors associated with complex poverty become causally interconnected and mutually reinforcing. The problems are made worse in the many instances in which poverty is racialized and those who are poor are subjected to various forms of racism. In Halifax, African-Canadians are disproportionately among the poor, and the experience of racism is a constant in their lives.[84] A 1957 study acknowledged: "It is only in certain parts of [North End Halifax], and not elsewhere in Halifax with the exception of Africville, that negro families can find housing accommodation."[85] It was only in 1955 that schools in Halifax were desegregated[86]; in the 1960s, many barber-shops and restaurants would not serve African-Canadians, and the stigmatization and stereotyping continue today.[87] In western Canada, it is Aboriginal people who are over-represented among the poor and who daily experience both face-to-face and systemic racism, as well as the related effects of colonialism.[88]

An understanding of colonialism is essential in developing a full appreciation of the complex poverty experienced by many Aboriginal people in rural, northern and urban communities. Aboriginal people were dispossessed of their lands, pushed onto reserves and thus excluded from the dominant culture and institutions of Canada and subjected to the colonial control of the *Indian Act* and the domination of the Indian agent. Tragically, many of their children were forcibly removed from their homes and confined in residential schools, where large numbers died. The children were subjected to abuse and were taught to be ashamed of who they and their families were. The purpose was to "kill the Indian in the child"[89] by preventing Aboriginal families from passing on their indigenous culture to their children. It was, and for many Canadians still is, justified on the false grounds that indigenous institutions and cultural and religious values are inferior to those of people of European origins. The resultant colonial ideology is all-pervasive. As Metis scholar Howard Adams put it:

> The characteristic form of colonialism then is a racial and economic hierarchy with an ideology that claims the superiority of the race and culture of the colonizer. This national ideology pervades colonial society and its institutions, such as schools, cultural agencies, the church and the media. ... the ideology becomes an inseparable part of perceived reality.[90]

Internalizing Poverty and Racism

Aboriginal people themselves may come to believe the all-pervasive notion that they are inferior. This is common among oppressed people and among those who experience complex poverty. "In fact, this process happens so frequently that it has a name, internalized oppression."[91] Or as Howard Adams puts it, many Aboriginal people "have internalized a colonized consciousness."[92] The results, as Aboriginal scholar Michael Hart argues, are devastating:

> Once Aboriginal persons internalize the colonization processes, we feel confused and powerless.... We may implode with overwhelming feelings of sadness or explode with feelings of anger. Some try to escape this state through alcohol, drugs and/or other forms of self-abuse.[93]

The consequence of internalizing the colonial ideology, the European-based assumption of Aboriginal inferiority, is often incapacitating: "Aboriginal people start to believe that we are incapable of learning and that the colonizers' degrading images and beliefs about Aboriginal people and our ways of being are true."[94]

A vicious cycle is set in motion: the assumption of Aboriginal peoples' inferiority becomes internalized by Aboriginal people themselves; in response, many lash out in self-abusive ways, reinforcing in the minds of the non-Aboriginal majority the assumptions of Aboriginal inferiority that lie at the heart of the colonial ideology. The more Aboriginal people move further into internalizing the colonization processes, "the more we degrade who we are as Aboriginal people." As Hart says, "All of these internalized processes only serve the colonizers, who then are able to sit back and say 'see, we were right.' In colonizers' eyes, the usurpation is justified."[95]

This deeper causal reality—what Dara Culhane has called the "mundane brutality of everyday poverty"[96]—is invisible to most non-Aboriginal people, who see only the outward, behaviourial manifestations of what Aboriginal people have internalized.

A very similar phenomenon is experienced by all those trapped in complex poverty. They are so frequently blamed for their poverty— on the grounds that their behaviour and cultural attributes are the cause of this poverty— that many come to believe it themselves. This can lead to a variety of psychologically debilitating outcomes related to self-esteem and self-confidence and a sense of hope for the future, which then make escape from poverty even more difficult.

A PERVERSE GOVERNMENTAL RESPONSE TO COMPLEX POVERTY

Governments have responded to this new form of complex poverty not by investing in anti-poverty strategies, but by incarcerating ever-larger numbers of the poor, and especially the racialized poor. At the very time that neoliberal policies have led to the dramatic cuts in social spending, these same governments have significantly increased their expenditures on prisons and imprisonment. In the U.S., it has been estimated that one young Black man in three is in prison or on probation or parole[97] and that the prison industry — what Angela Davis calls the "prison industrial complex"[98] — is now the third largest employer in the country.[99] In Chicago, to take but one example, 55 percent of the Black adult male population has a felony record.[100] Neoliberal governments have responded to the growth of complex poverty that their policies have done so much to create by punishing the poor. This follows logically and inexorably from the dominant way of explaining poverty — by blaming the poor themselves. If the poor are to blame for the poverty they experience, then they must be punished for their poverty-producing behaviour and cultural failings. The resultant and bitter irony is the "state policy of criminalization of the consequences of state-sponsored poverty."[101] In many racialized families that experience complex poverty, having a family member in prison has become normal. Alford Young found that for African-American men in Chicago's Near West Side, "jail formed a bigger part of their lives than did work" and "detention was talked about as if it were a common event in their lives."[102] In Oakland, California, Victor Rios asked forty Latino youth to write down the names of close friends and family members who were in prison. "All of them knew at least six people." All of the young men in his study "discussed prison as a familiar place."[103] The same is the case in Canada. Aboriginal people comprise 4 percent of Canada's population, but 23 percent of federal inmates, and "over the past ten years, the Aboriginal inmate population increased considerably by 37 percent while the non-Aboriginal inmate population increased only modestly by 2 percent."[104] Elizabeth Comack and her colleagues describe this phenomenon:

In Canada, prison has become for many young Aboriginal
people the contemporary equivalent of what the Indian residential school represented for their parents (Jackson 1989:
216). According to a one-day snapshot conducted in 2003,
Aboriginal youth were almost eight times more likely to be
in custody than were their non-Aboriginal counterparts. In
Manitoba, Aboriginal youth were sixteen times more likely
to be incarcerated than non-Aboriginal youth.[105]

The high level of incarceration is causally connected to the complex
racialized poverty experienced by so many Aboriginal people: families
have been deliberately undermined as a central aspect of the strategy of colonialism; appalling numbers of Aboriginal children are in
care — indeed, one can see Aboriginal history in terms of a succession
of various forms of institutionalization, from the residential schools,
to the "sixties scoop," to various forms of youth detention centres,
to the high rates of children in care and high rates of incarceration
in federal and provincial penal institutions.[106] Included amongst the
results is the fact that on average, Aboriginal children have lower literacy skills, and Aboriginal people generally have lower educational
outcomes, than the non-Aboriginal population, and "approximately
65–70 percent of prison inmates are unable to sufficiently read
and write."[107] The connections are obvious: complex poverty, and
especially racialized poverty, are at the root of a host of inter-related
problems, to which governments far too often respond by simply
locking up poor people, which then further damages families and
reinforces the destructive cycle of complex poverty.

All of these inter-related factors associated with complex poverty are likely to have profound psychological effects. These then
dramatically increase the likelihood that one will stay poor and, to

the extent that these attitudes are passed on to children, that poverty will be reproduced across generations. The consequence of all these inter-related factors is that poverty can trap people. The Canadian Centre for Policy Alternatives describes this phenomenon by using two metaphors:

> One is the notion of a complex web — a web of poverty, racism, drugs, gangs, violence. The other is the notion of a cycle — people caught in a cycle of inter-related problems. Both suggest the idea of people who are trapped, immobilized, unable to escape, destined to struggle with forces against which they cannot win, from which they cannot extricate themselves. The result is despair, resignation, anger, hopelessness, which then reinforces the cycle, and wraps them tighter in the web.[108]

Not only is this ethically unacceptable in a country as economically well off as Canada, but it is also exceptionally expensive. Thus, reducing poverty levels dramatically is for all Canadians both ethically appropriate and economically advantageous.

It is important, however, not to leave this chapter on a wholly negative note. It is true that complex poverty creates very difficult living conditions and that it can be hard for those caught in its web to extricate themselves. Nevertheless, in all very low-income communities there are strengths to be found, and many lives are lived in dignity, courage and generosity.[109] A part of the solution to complex poverty is to build on these strengths.

THE COSTS
OF POVERTY

I t is not possible to determine the financial costs of poverty in
Canada with precision. It is possible, however, to identify the
many ways in which poverty drives up costs to society and to governments and in some cases to estimate the magnitude of those costs.

Considering what poverty costs Canada in dollar terms may
seem like a cold and calculating approach to what many would more
properly see as a matter of social justice, of fairness. It is not fair, it
is not morally right, that so many people in a wealthy country like
Canada are poor, especially when a small minority has reaped a large
proportion of the benefits of economic growth in recent decades,
and especially when we have the capacity, if we were to choose to
do so, to reduce poverty in Canada to a fraction of its current level.
Nevertheless, it is the case that poverty imposes a large financial burden on the country as a whole, and for those not inclined to be moved
by appeals to fairness and social justice, perhaps the knowledge that
allowing poverty to persist is as expensive as it is — and almost certainly more expensive in the long run than the cost of dramatically
reducing poverty — will lead them to support anti-poverty measures.

Calculating the costs of poverty is a task that is in its relative
infancy and is fraught with methodological difficulties. Not a great

many studies attempting to estimate the costs of poverty have yet been done; those that have been done must of necessity rely upon a variety of assumptions, and these assumptions can be contested. The result is studies that produce estimates rather than precise costs. Different methods, with different assumptions, produce different estimates. Despite these limitations — fully acknowledged by the economists, and others, doing such calculations — the methods and assumptions and calculations are transparent and can be understood by non-economists. This means that it is possible for any interested and reasonably intelligent person to examine these studies and reach their own conclusions in regards to their plausibility and accuracy. And it means that we are beginning to get an informed sense of the real dollar costs of poverty to Canada. What we find is that poverty imposes very large economic costs, not just on those who are poor — although obviously they bear the brunt of the burden, financial and otherwise, of poverty — but also on society at large and on governments.

Governments and policy makers are not designing budgets with these costs in mind. Part of the challenge is that investments in anti-poverty strategies would have to be large and they would have to be made first, while the benefits in terms of cost reductions and increased economic activity and tax revenues — described below — would come later. The time lag is an issue for governments facing various fiscal constraints and seeking to be re-elected. This is especially the case when so many citizens blame the poor for their poverty, which means that politicians and political parties believe there would be little electoral support for investments in an anti-poverty strategy, the up-front costs of which would be large. Further, as can be seen in the case of the current environmental crisis, governments are not as effective as they need to be in acting in the long term. Nevertheless, this exercise in identifying the costs of poverty is important because it shows that poverty is expensive and that it would make good financial sense — for all of us, not just those of us who are poor — to invest for the purpose of dramatically reducing poverty.

HEALTH, CRIME AND OPPORTUNITY COSTS OF POVERTY

One particular methodology developed by Nathan Laurie in Ontario and replicated in British Columbia and other provinces by the Canadian Centre for Policy Alternatives and others calculates the estimated costs of poverty in three realms: the added costs to the health care system because of poverty; the added costs of crime because of poverty; and foregone economic output, including foregone government tax revenues — what economists call "opportunity costs" — because of poverty. These studies are cautious in saying that while the reasons *why* or the precise ways in which poverty produces poor health outcomes or an increased incidence of crime, for example, are not fully understood or agreed upon, nevertheless it is clear that poverty is causally associated with poor health outcomes and a higher incidence of crime and that poverty does reduce future economic activity and thus government revenues.

This methodology produces a conservative estimate of the costs of poverty because it does not include all the costs of poverty. For example, it does not include the costs of homelessness. To calculate the costs of poverty, this method divides all people in a jurisdiction — a country, province or city — into quintiles, that is, into five equally sized groups arranged by income, and makes the assumption that those in the lowest income quintile are those in poverty. What is found is that, considering health costs for example, those in the lowest income quintile use the health care system more, and thus cost the health care system more, than those in the second income quintile. This is consistent with the repeated findings of those who study the social determinants of health: there is a gradient in the effects of income inequality, such that on average, the lower the income the worse the health outcomes, and thus the higher the costs to the health care system.[1] Those in the lowest income quintile cost the health care system the most. The method moves on to calculate the savings in health costs if all those in the lowest income quintile were to be moved to the second income quintile and were to use the health system to the same — lesser — extent as those in the second income quintile. The amount by which health care costs would be reduced is deemed to be the extra health care costs attributable to poverty. In the cases of Manitoba[2] and Saskatchewan,[3] for example, the extra costs of health care were 6.7 percent and 6 percent respectively of total health care costs in those provinces. The cost of the additional health care usage by those in B.C.'s lowest income quintile has been calculated at 6.7 percent of total health care costs in the province, which amounts to $1.2 billion per year.[4]

Extrapolating to Canada as a whole, the cost of poverty in terms of higher health care costs is $9.1 billion per year. In other words, those in the lowest income quintile cost Canada's health care system $9.1 billion per year more than do the same number of people in the second income quintile. Or we could express this slightly differently by saying that the amount that Canadians would save in health care costs by eliminating poverty — in this case, by increasing the incomes of all those in the lowest income quintile to the average level of those in the second-lowest income quintile — would be $9.1 billion per year.

The same method calculates the increased costs of crime and the lost revenues to governments because those in the lowest income quintile earn lower incomes than, or are not as actively involved in the labour force as, those in the second income quintile. Including these costs along with higher health care costs, economist Iglika Ivanova calculates the total cost of poverty in British Columbia at between $8.1 billion and $9.2 billion in 2008.[5] This amount is double the cost of a comprehensive anti-poverty strategy in B.C.[6] Since B.C.'s population in 2013 is approximately 13 percent of the total population in Canada, we can estimate the cost of poverty in Canada as a whole — at least in regards to higher costs related to health care, crime and reduced economic activity and lower tax revenues because of poverty — as being approximately $62.4 to $70.8 billion per year.

THE COSTS OF LOW-INCOME HOUSING AND HOMELESSNESS

The above figure does not include the costs of homelessness. *The State of Homelessness in Canada 2013* estimates that "at least 200,000 Canadians access homeless emergency services or sleep outside in a given year, ... as many as 1.3 million Canadians have experienced homelessness or extremely insecure housing at some point during the past five years" and 30,000 Canadians are homeless on any given night. As long ago as 1998, the City of Toronto declared homelessness to be a "national emergency."[7] In the U.S. and Canada, the strategy for dealing with homelessness is reactive and relies on emergency services and law enforcement initiatives that are expensive. Although there are limitations to the various studies that attempt to estimate the costs of homelessness — for example, data are often difficult to access and some studies may overstate by extrapolating the costs of chronic, high-needs cases to all homeless cases — nevertheless the costs of our reliance on emergency-based responses are high. Homeless people, and even more so the chronically homeless, incur much higher costs than people who are housed, especially for emergency room visits, hospitalization, emergency shelters, policing costs and costs related to more frequent imprisonment. In fact, health conditions are so bad for homeless people that they are eight to ten times more likely to die than housed people of the same age.[8] Stephen Gaetz, who has conducted many studies of homelessness, observes: "Homelessness incurs staggering health costs measured in terms of increased illness, use of health services and early death."[9] For example, a 2008 Calgary study found that the cost of homelessness amounted to $72,444 per year for a transiently homeless person and $134,642 per year for a chronically homeless person, while the cost

"Boarded up house, I don't know, looks bad on the community. Just lazy not caring people. Sell it. The city should invest in this and renovate it and make money from it because people need housing. But, instead it looks bad on the hood. It probably was a party house or crack shack. You can tell bad stuff happened here." — Photo and caption by an inner-city youth.

Source: *Canadian Centre for Policy Alternatives-Manitoba (ccpa-mb), 2013,* A Youth Lens on Poverty in Winnipeg: State of the Inner City Report 2013, *Winnipeg, ccpa-mb, p. 30*

of housing and supports for a chronically homeless person would be $10,000–$25,000 per year.[10] A British Columbia study calculated the cost of homelessness for the almost 12,000 people in that province suffering with severe addictions and/or mental illness and who were "absolutely homeless" at $55,000 per person per year, and estimated the cost of an alternative strategy of providing housing and supports to homeless persons at $37,000 per year, a savings of $18,000 per person per year, and $211 million per year in total.[11] The estimated average monthly cost of keeping a homeless person in Toronto in a shelter is estimated at $1,932, in a provincial jail at $4,333 and in a hospital bed at $10,900.[12] By contrast, using the alternative strategy of finding housing and providing supports for a homeless person costs much less: rent supplements are $701 per month and social housing costs $200 per month. Steve Pomeroy, in his four-city study of the costs of homelessness, shows the following costs per homeless person per year: prison or psychiatric hospital, $66,000–$120,000; emergency shelters, $13,000–$42,000.[13] By contrast, supportive and transitional housing would cost $13,000–$18,000, while affordable housing without supports would be $5000–$8000. Again, the cost of providing housing with supports for those who are homeless is far less expensive than our current reliance upon expensive emergency services.

CRIME COSTS OF POVERTY

As with so much else having to do with poverty, the relationship between homelessness and prison is often a vicious cycle: a large proportion (one estimate is 22 percent) of those imprisoned were homeless when arrested; in turn, a large proportion of those released from prison (one estimate is 32 percent) soon become homeless because of the lack of supports for them upon release.[14] A study by the John Howard Society of Toronto and the University of Toronto referred to men "caught in a revolving door between jails and shelters" and found that 85 percent of those in the study who were among the incarcerated homeless "anticipated being homeless again upon discharge."[15]

This is a problem for many reasons, not least because the cost of keeping someone in prison is so high. According to the Parliamentary Budget Office, the average cost of keeping an inmate in a provincial cell is $84,225 per year, and in a federal cell it is $147,467. Despite such high costs, capital spending on the prison system — that is, building new and expanding existing prisons — is estimated to grow from $246.8 million in 2009–10, to $506 million in 2011–2.[16] In financial terms, it appears that we would be better off spending this money on finding supported housing for those released from prison. In fact, a study by the John Howard Society of Toronto found that when this is done, the likelihood of reoffending is reduced, resulting in savings to the system amounting to $350,000 per person over

The homelessness-prison-homelessness cycle

a lifetime.[17] Putting homeless people in prison, and building ever more prisons in order to do so, is expensive; if instead we were to pay the costs to move homeless people into supportive housing, and to provide similar housing services upon release from prison, the costs to society as a whole would be reduced, and the lives of those who would otherwise be imprisoned would be improved.

Similarly, it has been found that issuing tickets to homeless people for panhandling and sleeping in a public park is not only ineffectual but also expensive. Bill O'Grady of the University of Guelph and his colleagues found that in Toronto, tickets issued under the *Safe Streets Act* of 2000 rose from 710 in 2000 to 15,324 in 2010.[18] The total cost of the tickets issued over that eleven-year period was over $4 million. But only $8,000 was ever paid, and the cost to the Toronto Police Service of issuing the tickets that produced $8,000 in revenues was estimated at almost $1 million. This makes no financial sense whatsoever.

What these findings demonstrate is that there are large policing and imprisonment costs associated with our current reactive and emergency-based approach to homelessness, and these costs could be significantly reduced by a "housing first" strategy — i.e., finding housing for homeless people and then providing them with the supports they need to improve their circumstances. The *National At Home/Chez Soi Final Report* describes the results of the large, cross-Canada research study of the housing first approach.[19] The Report found that there are cost savings — reduced health system usage, and especially reductions in the numbers of days spent in hospital — that follow from the housing first approach. For every $10 invested, there were savings of $9.60 for high needs participants and $3.42 for moderate needs participants over a two-year period. For the 10 percent of partipants with the highest needs, the savings were calculated at $21.72 for every $10 invested.[20]

A preponderance of studies in Australia and the U.S. as well as Canada found that it is far less expensive to provide homeless people with housing and supports than it is to do nothing about homelessness.[21] The result of doing nothing is that the homeless rely upon expensive emergency services. In the vast majority of studies, the costs of allowing homelessness to persist are found to be higher than the costs of earlier, preventative interventions.

COSTS OF CHILD POVERTY

Child poverty is even more expensive. The loss of future income tax revenue to Canada because of the intergenerational impact of child poverty is put by one estimate at $3.1 to $3.8 billion per year.[22] A study of the costs of child poverty in the U.S. that used statistical relationships between childhood poverty and outcomes as adults estimated not only the opportunity costs of reduced levels of economic activity, but also the added health care and crime costs. It found those costs to be at least $500 billion per year, which is 3.8 percent of the U.S.'s GDP,[23] while a similar study in the U.K. found that child poverty costs £25 billion, or 2 percent of GDP.[24] The costs of child poverty are particularly difficult to estimate because these costs — poorer health, higher incidence of troubles with the law, lower educational outcomes and thus more poorly paid jobs or no jobs at all — are realized well into the future. Nevertheless, child poverty is a serious problem in Canada and it has repeatedly been shown to produce many negative outcomes.

Child poverty is really about family poverty, and one potential aspect of the poverty experienced by families in Canada is family breakdown, leading to the apprehension of their children by child welfare authorities and the placement of those children "in care" — in a foster home or group home or other institutional setting. We know that a high proportion of youth who have been in care end up being homeless — some recent estimates find that between 41 percent and 43 percent of homeless youth in Canada had previously been in foster care or group homes[25] and that "children and adolescents comprise the fastest growing segment of the homeless population in Canada."[26]

Not only is homelessness costly, especially when compared to a housing first alternative, but so too is placing children in care in the first place. Journalist Catherine Mitchell reports that in Manitoba alone, the number of children in care (more than 80 percent of whom are Aboriginal) has risen from 5,782 in 2004 to 9,800 in 2012, during which time the budget for child welfare in Manitoba has grown by 350 percent, to $403 million, a growth rate higher than that for the costs of health care, leading Mitchell to ask, "Is child welfare the new health care, the insatiable black hole of the [provincial] budget?"[27] Again, society as a whole pays a high and growing cost for our failure to invest in effective anti-poverty strategies, and since such a high proportion of these ever-growing numbers of children and youth in care will end up being homeless, we can see that yet again, poverty produces a cycle — from poverty, to placement in care, to homelessness, to poor health and low educational outcomes, to poorly paid jobs or no jobs at all, and thus more poverty. In this, as in so many other ways, the costs of poverty are reproduced over and over again.

EDUCATIONAL OUTCOME COSTS

As was shown in Chapter 4, poverty produces poor educational outcomes. Those who have lower levels of formal education are more likely to experience poverty, and those in poverty are more likely to have low educational levels, producing a poverty-education cycle. This is costly. A study by the Toronto-Dominion Bank observes: "Poor educational outcomes are costing the country hundreds of billions of dollars in lost opportunity."[28] Focusing on Aboriginal people, who comprise a large and rapidly growing proportion of western Canada's population, economist Sonya Gulati refers to a study that found that "65% of First Nations peoples in urban Saskatchewan who have at least Level 3 literacy are employed. The same employment rate for those scoring below Level 3 is 31%."[29] Those with low levels of literacy are less likely — half as likely in the case of this study — to be employed. We know that on average, Aboriginal people have lower formal educational levels and lower employment rates than the population at large. Eliminating this education/employment gap could increase Canada's economic output by as much as $401 billion and Canada's tax revenues by $39 billion over the twenty-five-year period from 2001 to 2026.[30] The alternative — failing to invest in improved Aboriginal educational outcomes — is a contributing factor in the very high rates of incarceration experienced by Aboriginal people. Far from investing in Aboriginal education, we are under-investing. Former prime minister of Canada Paul Martin estimated that on-reserve schools are under-funded by $2000–$3000 per student, compared to Canadian schools generally.[31] The consequences are both predictable and costly. While Aboriginal people comprise 4 percent of Canada's population, they constitute 23 percent of federal inmates, and 70 percent of inmates entering federal custody have less than grade 8 literacy levels.[32] Poor educational outcomes are a product of poverty and contribute to the reproduction of poverty and, especially in the case of the racialized poor, contribute to increased rates of incarceration, which is an exceptionally costly form of housing.

WHEN WE DO INVEST IN SOLUTIONS, THERE ARE COST SAVINGS

Investing in improved educational outcomes appears to be cost effective. Pathways to Education, the high school support program that started more than a decade ago in Toronto's Regent Park, has dramatically increased high school graduation rates and admissions to post-secondary education in that low-income community. Results for 2011 at Pathways' Regent Park program show a reduction in dropout rates of more than 70 percent and an increased participation in post-secondary education and training of more than 300 percent.[33] This will produce significant future savings and increased economic output, and thus tax revenues. A Sault Ste. Marie study found that over a forty-year working life, those with a university degree earned almost $1 million more than someone with just a high school diploma,[34] and thus they would produce more tax revenues, which in turn could be used to our collective benefit. The Urban Circle Training Centre, a highly effective Aboriginal adult education program in Winnipeg's low-income North End, has an 85–90 percent success rate — which means that students previously on some form of government assistance graduate from the program they are taking and find jobs related to that program — and they estimate that Urban Circle saved taxpayers, by a conservative calculation, a cumulative total of $53.5 million from 1990 to 2010.[35] The authors of a U.S. study concluded, "If we made high-quality pre-kindergarten programs universally available to children, the expected returns over time might easily dwarf the costs," potentially amounting to an annual increase in GDP of 3.7 percent, which is significant since, as seen above, this team of economists estimated the total costs of child poverty in the U.S. at 3.8 percent of GDP.[36]

Investing in early childhood education and care (ECEC) is also cost effective. It is well established that children do better in school when they arrive well prepared for kindergarten. In low-income areas, a high proportion of children are ill prepared to start school. Early development instrument (EDI) scores for B.C. and Manitoba show that on average, children in low-income areas are much less well prepared for school than are children who grow up in more economically stable areas.[37] Those children who are poorly prepared to start school are less likely to succeed in school and more likely as a result to earn low incomes and/or be in conflict with the law. The long-term costs can be high.

The TD Bank has called for public investment in ECEC on the grounds that doing so would be "beneficial for children, parents as well as the broader economy."[38] In their *Alternative Federal Budget*, The Canadian Centre for Policy Alternatives point out the benefits of ECEC:

> There is compelling evidence that public investment in early childhood education and care — with its multiple benefits to multiple groups — offers among the highest benefits that nations can adopt. Studies have repeatedly shown that well-designed public spending on ECEC promotes health, advances women's equality, addresses child and family poverty, deepens social inclusion, and grows the economy.[39]

We have lots of evidence that every dollar invested in ECEC earns more than a dollar in the future. If we are able to estimate the financial benefits of public investment in ECEC, we can conclude that the costs of a failure to invest in ECEC are the foregone benefits that such investment would otherwise have produced.

Such estimates vary but all are clear on the cost savings. One suggests that investments in early childhood education for low-income children — most studies suggest that children from low-income families benefit most from ECEC — can produce from $4 to $16 for every dollar invested,[40] while another reported, "for every dollar spent on early childhood education, the benefits range from $1.49 to $2.78." U.S. studies "estimate benefits to be as high as $17 for every dollar spent, although the programs analyzed were solely for disadvantaged children."[41]

In Manitoba, each dollar invested in ECEC produces a return of $1.38 to the Winnipeg economy.[42] Martha Friendly and Susan Prentice, well-established authorities on childcare, refer to more than seventy studies in the U.S. that confirm that "every $1 of childcare spending creates positive local ripples as dollars move through the local economy," amounting on average to $1.49 for every dollar spent on childcare.[43] The relatively strong childcare system in Quebec benefits mothers in particular. Such a system enables them to participate to a much greater extent in the labour force than mothers elsewhere, helping them to pull their families out of poverty.

These estimates of the benefits of investment in ECEC vary, depending upon methods used and the particularities of each case. But the variance in these estimates should not obscure the main conclusion, which is that investment in ECEC produces benefits that outweigh the costs; there are multiple beneficiaries; and children in low-income families, and their lone-parent mothers, benefit most. The cost of not investing in ECEC is the loss of all these benefits.

POVERTY IS EXPENSIVE

The costs of poverty in Canada are high. Although those costs cannot be calculated with precision, we know that poverty — and especially complex poverty — produces poor health outcomes, poor

Public Costs & Benefits
High/Scope Perry Preschool Program

(Constant 2,000 dollars, 3% discount rate)

Total Benefits $195,621

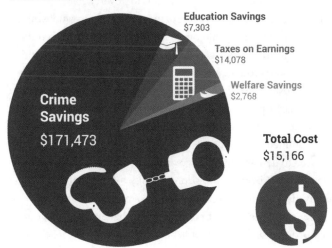

Education Savings
$7,303

Taxes on Earnings
$14,078

Welfare Savings
$2,768

Crime Savings

$171,473

Total Cost
$15,166

Investment
For every $1 spent,
there are $12.90 in benefits

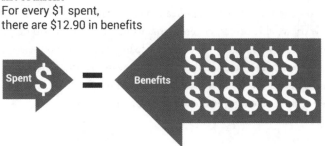

Source: <http://www.highscope.org/content.asp?ContentId=219>

educational outcomes, higher incidences of crime and incarceration and significantly reduced levels of economic activity and thus tax revenues. Some sophisticated analyses of these costs find them to be very high. It follows that it would make good financial— as well as ethical— sense to invest in solutions to poverty.

It is true that the up-front cost of those investments would be substantial. The benefits would outweigh the costs and would continue to outweigh the costs well into the future, so that investments in poverty would produce a very attractive "rate of return." But governments whose approach is shaped by neoliberalism are not prepared to make large public investments— especially investments aimed at low-income people and communities— when the benefits will not be immediately realized. And Canadians have not so far been prepared to demand that our governments make such investments, at least in part because they do not really believe that poverty can be solved— despite the clear evidence of much lower poverty rates in other countries— and because so many believe that the poor are not worthy of such investments because they are the cause of their own poverty.

We can solve poverty, and it would make good economic sense to do so. But to make the significant public investments that solving poverty would require, governments would have to abandon their neoliberal approach. They would have to make different political and public policy choices than they have, for the most part, been making in the past thirty to forty years. This would require that Canadians demand that their governments make these choices.

6

SOLUTIONS
THAT WORK

We know what to do to defeat poverty. But we don't do it. The problem is not that we lack the knowledge; the problem is that we lack the political will. Our governments choose not to make public investments in the solutions that would wrestle poverty to the ground. And Canadians as a whole do not demand that our governments make public investments in those solutions. In the absence of the implementation of a well-designed and well-funded poverty reduction plan, poverty will continue to be reproduced. The status quo is unacceptably high levels of poverty.

Part of the problem is that over the past thirty-plus years governments around the world — Canada included — have adopted, to a greater or lesser extent, the ideology and policies of neoliberalism. Neoliberalism — which accentuates the worst tendencies of capitalism — has served to widen the gap between the rich and the rest of us and has in most important respects worsened the problem of poverty in Canada. Neoliberalism's internal logic is such that as long as it persists, so too will high levels of poverty.

Another part of the problem is that many Canadians blame the existence of poverty on the poor themselves. That is the "easier" explanation and the explanation favoured by the media. The dominant form of public discourse involving poverty is *not* an ongoing discussion of the high costs of poverty and the benefits to all of anti-poverty initiatives; rather the discourse is disproportionately some form or other of "poor-bashing" or appeals to charity. As long as the poor are thought to be the cause of their own problems, mounting the political pressure needed to force governments to invest in anti-poverty strategies will not be possible.

Poverty can be solved, and we will all be better off when it is solved. But in order for it to be solved governments will need to invest in the various elements of a coherent poverty reduction plan — and will need to do so in significant amounts and consistently year after year over at least a generation — and we as Canadian citizens need to insist that our governments make these investments. If we do not, poverty will persist long into the future, with all the damage that it does to individuals and families, to communities and to the Canadian economy and society as a whole. There is no doubt that with the kinds of policies and programs that governments could and should adopt, and that are described below, poverty would be reduced to a fraction of its current level.

A POVERTY REDUCTION PLAN

Eight of the ten provinces in Canada have adopted poverty reduction plans (B.C. and Saskatchewan have not); a House of Commons committee recommended in November 2010 "that the federal government join with the provinces to introduce an action plan for reducing poverty in Canada"[1]; some cities — Ottawa and Calgary, among others — have introduced such strategies, and some non-governmental organizations have also developed such plans.[2] Even though in most cases these poverty reduction plans have not been fully, or in some cases even partially, implemented, the fact that so many governments have seen fit to prepare poverty reduction plans is a good thing. If we are to make dramatic reductions to poverty in Canada, we need to approach the problem in a systematic and coherent fashion. We need a plan.

A good poverty reduction plan would have a number of specific features.[3] First, it would be the product of broad and genuine consultations with the public, including especially those who are living in poverty and whose experiential knowledge is essential in designing an effective plan.

Second, it would include targets, timelines and specific, measurable indicators. For example, the plan might say that the rate of poverty as measured by the after-tax low income cut-off (LICO) will be reduced by one-third, from its current rate of x percent to y percent, by March 31, 2015, and it might say that a specific number of social housing units will be built by December 31, 2015. A range of such targets, timelines and indicators would be included in a good plan.

Third, a good plan would include some specific accountability mechanisms. For example, a senior cabinet minister should be responsible for the implementation and the outcomes of the plan and for producing an annual report that measures outcomes against targets and timelines and that is tabled in the provincial legislature or federal House of Commons and made widely available to the public. Some plans are incorporated in legislation — Quebec's *Act to Combat Poverty and Social Exclusion*, passed in 2002, is a good example. A public advisory committee with the mandate to oversee the implementation of the plan and to draw attention to gaps between targets, timelines and outcomes would also improve accountability.

Fourth, the plan would have to be comprehensive and take a long-term approach. Poverty is complex and multi-faceted. It includes, among other characteristics, not only a shortage of money but also inadequate housing, low levels of education, lack of attachment to the labour market or employment in low-waged and insecure precarious jobs, concerns about safety and security in the community, low levels of self-esteem and self-confidence and even in some cases a sense of hopelessness about the future. There is no single, simple or short-term solution for this kind of poverty. Therefore a good poverty reduction plan would include policy measures and programs with identifiable targets and timelines — both short- and long-term — and measurable indicators that address, for example, housing, education, social assistance rates, job creation and strategies for moving low-income people into good jobs, and so on. And a good plan would adopt the approach that expenditures in these areas are in fact productive investments in our collective future, and it would be explained to the public in such terms.

Fifth, while a specific cabinet minister should be accountable for all aspects of the plan and its outcomes, the implementation of the plan should include a "whole of government" approach. This means that most government departments and programs would have specific responsibilities, and related targets and timelines, and all departments and programs would work on the plan in a coordinated and cross-departmental fashion with a view to the long term.

Sixth, a good poverty reduction plan would include a focus on those groups of people who are most marginalized and most likely to be mired in the web of complex poverty —Aboriginal people, newcomers, single parents, for example. Consistent with this, the plan would recognize and respond to the fact that poverty is racialized and gendered and frequently spatially concentrated. A primary focus of a good plan is to develop human capacity and capability, especially that of the least advantaged among us.

No single poverty reduction plan currently meets all of these standards, although both Quebec and Newfoundland and Labrador have strong plans that appear to have produced some good results to date. Most provincial poverty reduction plans include at least some of the positive features listed above. But the existence of these plans — despite their various weaknesses[4] and despite the continued reliance on neoliberal policies by most governments in Canada — is nevertheless important, in large part because they could play an important role in public education.

The existence of poverty reduction plans could raise people's consciousness about the problem of poverty and could combat the widely held view that poverty is the fault of the poor and that

"It's a garden where kids garden. It keeps kids busy. It's a handy skill. It exists because there aren't many kids' gardens and it offers fresh food." — Photo and caption by an inner-city youth.

Source: CCPA-MB, 2013, A Youth Lens on Poverty in Winnipeg: State of the Inner City Report 2013, Winnipeg, p. 35

therefore we need not and should not take any action to reduce poverty. A good poverty reduction plan for Canada, one that includes targets, timelines, indicators and accountability mechanisms, would promote public debate about the issue, and this alone would be a big step forward in the struggle against poverty, because it could lead to Canadians demanding that our governments invest in anti-poverty strategies.

A particularly exciting outcome of such a public debate would be if the media were to begin to produce daily reports on poverty indicators in the same fashion that they now produce daily reports on financial and especially stock market indicators. Every day, CBC, for example, tells its listeners and viewers the amounts by which the Toronto Stock Exchange and the New York Stock Exchange and the value of the Canadian dollar relative to the American dollar have gone up or down. It would be an enormously valuable public service and a huge step in the direction of social justice if CBC and other media outlets were to report also on poverty reduction indicators. The following are examples of ways in which the media might, on various days, report on poverty reduction indicators:

> The number of social housing units constructed in New Brunswick in the year ending March 31 was 440. This is an increase of 10 percent over the previous year and represents 88 percent of the year's target of 500 new units. Opposition members in the Legislature are demanding to know why, for the second year in a row, the government has failed to meet the target set out in the provincial poverty reduction plan. Housing advocacy groups in the province are demonstrating in front of the constituency office of the minister responsible for the poverty reduction plan, claiming that far too many

people in the province are still suffering the many ill effects of living in core housing need.

According to the latest count, taken November 1 of this year, the number of homeless people in Canada is 24,000, a reduction of 20 percent relative to the 30,000 homeless recorded on November 1 of last year. Governments across the country are attributing this positive change to the widespread implementation in most large cities of housing first policies and are stating that the cost savings resulting from lower use of emergency services by homeless people will more than offset the costs associated with the housing first programs.

The number of Aboriginal people in Manitoba who earned their grade 12 diploma in the year ending June 30 is 650, which represents a gain of 18 percent over last year's 550 graduates. The provincial poverty reduction plan called for 600 Aboriginal grade 12 graduates this year, so that the target was exceeded by 50 graduates, or 8 percent. The Minister in charge of the plan has attributed this success to her government's significant investments in adult learning centres located in low-income communities.

The annual food bank count found that the number of Canadians using food banks in the latest year was 750,000, a reduction of over 100,000, or 13 percent, from last year's total of 850,000. Anti-poverty activists are attributing this gain to two things: first, that six of ten provincial govern-ments increased the housing component of their social assistance rates by the amount set out in their poverty reduction plans, so that those on social assistance have not had to use their food budget to pay the rent, which in past years has forced them to rely on food banks; and second, that eight of ten provinces have increased their minimum wages to a level such that a full-time worker paid the minimum wage earns at least enough to be above the after-tax LICO.

The government of Ontario today announced the opening of three new childcare centres with a total of 140 spaces. This brings the total of new childcare spaces created this year to 950, falling just short of the target of 1000 new spaces set out in the poverty reduction plan. Media outlets across the country have been critical of Ontario, as well as other provincial governments, for falling short of their poverty reduction plan targets for new childcare spaces, pointing to the well-known fact that the long-term costs of failing to invest in children are greater than the cost of investing in our future now.

If the media in Canada were to report in a systematic way, as described above, on the outcomes of poverty reduction plans, it would contribute to a much enlarged public awareness of poverty and of the steps that need to be taken to significantly reduce poverty. The Canadian public would know what is working well and what is not. Canadians would be able to see that public investments were producing positive results. This in turn would increase the pressure for still more public investment in those strategies that have been shown to work well in reducing poverty.

CANADIANS' ATTITUDES ABOUT POVERTY

At the moment, most Canadians believe that poverty simply cannot be solved, that the problem is too overwhelming. Most Canadians see themselves as "middle class," and they are worried about their own economic circumstances — and quite rightly, given the growing gap between the rich and the rest of us. Canadians are concerned about their growing levels of personal indebtedness and fear that the "intergenerational bargain" — the deeply held assumption, and hope, that our children and grandchildren will do as well as we did, or better — is slipping away. Most Canadians see the poor as the "Other" and place the blame for poverty on poor people themselves — the blame the victim approach — or they are simply indifferent, caught up as they are in their own day-to-day concerns. All of this makes the development of an effective anti-poverty strategy particularly difficult.

Yet at the same time Canadians see themselves as being, and have aspirations to be, a caring society. Research done by Trish Hennessey of the Canadian Centre for Policy Alternatives shows that Canadians want leadership from their prime ministers and premiers in the development of specific plans to create opportunities for people who are poor:

> In an Environics poll taken in the fall of 2008, 90 percent of Canadians said they wanted the federal government to take leadership in reducing poverty. In virtually equal numbers (89 percent), they called for the Prime Minister and the Premiers to set targets and timelines to achieve this objective.[5]

Other polls consistently show this high level of support — 80 percent and more — for actions to reduce poverty. This widely felt desire could be the basis upon which to build an effective anti-poverty strategy.

A POVERTY REDUCTION PLAN FOR CANADA

Poverty is a major problem in Canada, and while it can be solved, it cannot easily be solved. Poverty is widespread, deep and complex; it is often intergenerational; it disproportionately affects specific groups of people; and it imposes large costs on all of us — costs that exceed the cost of solving the problem. Solving the problem of poverty requires a systematic and comprehensive poverty reduction plan with the characteristics described above. And the plan needs to do more than make minor adjustments to existing policies. It needs to be bold. In preparing a proposed poverty reduction plan for Manitoba, the CCPA-MB "heard loud and clear ... that minor adjustments to existing policies and programs are insufficient and the Province must undertake comprehensive and systematic action to reduce poverty."[6]

What follows is a brief description of the kinds of initiatives that are needed to reduce poverty dramatically in Canada. Some of these policies and programs would benefit all Canadians, directly or indirectly, and therefore could — with proper government explanations — meet with broad public support. These policies include, for example, a national childcare strategy, a national housing strategy and various educational initiatives. Other policies would be targeted more narrowly at those most marginalized — as recommended in all strong poverty reduction plans. It is likely that these too would find broad support among the Canadian public *if* governments were to make the case for a strong poverty reduction plan in an open and honest fashion, making it clear that this is what a caring society should do and that we all benefit, including financially, if poverty is dramatically reduced.

It is important to note that the approach to poverty reduction described below does not include any of the various kinds of charitable initiatives that are so common today. Well-intentioned people respond positively to charitable appeals — bringing something for the food bank to a hockey game is a common one — but charity responds to symptoms; it does not get to the roots of problems. Charity does not contribute to the structural change that we need if poverty is to be dramatically reduced. Charitable donations rather than structural change are favoured by those who benefit most from the growing levels of inequality in Canada. When the wealthy make large charitable donations, as many do, they set the conditions under which they will give, typically getting the public credit and recognition and earning a tax break. This approach, while advantageous for those able to afford large donations, will never solve poverty in Canada. We can solve poverty, or at least dramatically reduce the incidence of poverty, difficult though that will be, only by making significant, strategic public investments.

A JOB CREATION STRATEGY

Poverty exists when people do not have good jobs, and it is particular groups of people — Aboriginal people, single mothers, racialized minorities, for example — who are least likely to hold good jobs. Because a good job is a way out of poverty, a job creation strategy would need to be a central part of a poverty reduction plan. At the heart of a good job creation strategy is building things that Canada needs, hiring people to do the building and related work, and in particular hiring from those groups of people most detached from the labour market.

Canada needs infrastructure — flood prevention in the face of climate change, repair, maintenance and replacement of sewage and water systems and rapid transit in major Canadian cities, for example. Canada would also benefit enormously from a green jobs strategy — retrofitting public buildings and older residential homes would not only benefit the environment, but also create very large numbers of jobs, and the cost of creating those jobs and doing that work would be paid back in a relatively short period out of the resulting energy savings. Everyone would benefit. Hiring and training Aboriginal people in green jobs in Winnipeg's inner city, for example, has produced a significant ripple effect: "Successful trainees are often proud to become positive figures in their children's lives ... [and] this can help break the cycle of family poverty."[7] An effective poverty reduction plan would include a national housing and a national childcare strategy; the building associated with these initiatives would also create large numbers of jobs.

Governments also hire relatively large numbers of people on an ongoing basis, even in these neoliberal times, and this hiring capacity could be used to hire people from groups that have historically been marginalized — people with disabilities, visible minorities and Aboriginal people, for example. Governments and government agencies typically offer unionized jobs that pay reasonable wages and offer benefits and some job security.

Much has been learned about moving low-income people into good jobs.[8] Of particular benefit would be the use of a labour market intermediary (LMI). LMIs are public bodies that bring together five types of institutions and organizations — community-based organizations that work in low-income areas with marginalized people; governments; educational institutions; trade unions; and employers. These five would bring together all the requisite skills and knowledge—the barriers to employment faced by poor people, the training and education they might need and the jobs that are available, for example— to facilitate their collective purpose, which is the movement of otherwise marginalized people into these new jobs.[9]

The combination of these two measures — building things that Canadians need, such as infrastructure, housing and childcare, and ensuring that among those hired to do the building and all the related work are the large numbers of Canadians now detached from the labour market— would be a major step toward the elimination of poverty. And all Canadians would benefit, not only from the cost savings that would arise when the numbers in poverty are reduced, but also from their use of the things that would be built in this process.

MINIMUM WAGE AND LIVING WAGE

It is a good job that lifts people out of poverty, and among other things, a good job means wages that are high enough to bring workers above the poverty line. The large number of Canadians living in poverty is caused primarily by low wages . One important means of addressing this is to increase the legislated minimum wage — doing so is largely a provincial responsibility— to a level such that no single person working a full-year, full-time job lives in poverty, and then linking the minimum wage to the cost of living so that it automatically increases over time.

Some have argued that increasing the legislated minimum wage will lead employers to hire fewer workers, eroding its effectiveness as part of a poverty reduction strategy. However, the weight of the evidence is that reasonable increases in the minimum wage, and especially increases that can be anticipated and planned for by employers, as would be the case if the minimum wage automatically increased with increases in the cost of living, would have no discernible effect on total employment.[10]

A strong minimum wage policy is not only an important anti-poverty tool. It also produces broader economic benefits. For example, higher minimum wages are likely to benefit employers by reducing employee turnover and its associated costs. More broadly, those workers benefitting from a strong minimum wage policy are likely to spend all of their wages in the local economy, thus producing a positive multiplier effect. A study by the Federal Reserve Bank of Chicago "found that a $1 increase in the minimum wage results, on average, in $2800 in new spending by affected households in the following year."[11] This spending supports local economies. Since

Decent wages buy cars: Henry Ford's wage policy
Henry Ford was the greatest employer in the world. He despised unions, but, unlike almost all corporate employers nowadays, he knew decent wages were actually good. With decent pay turnover went way down, productivity went way up, but, just as importantly, decently-paid workers could buy things, especially cars. His "strategy" of paying decent wages paid off handsomely for Ford Inc.—profits went up, production and productivity went up. And, the price of a Model T went down from about $500 in 1914 down to $240 in 1925. In 1914, Ford autoworkers made $5 per day and had to work 100 days to buy a Model T. In 1925, they had to work less than 50 days. In 2014, a Ford autoworker, paid the starting wage of $16-an-hour wage has to work 110 days just to afford the least expensive car they make, and close to 200 days for a mid-range Ford!

Source: Toby Sanger, 2014, "Henry Ford's Argument with Stephen Harper," TheTyee.ca, January 9. At <thetyee.ca/Opinion/2014/01/08/Henry-Fords-Argument-with-Stephen-Harper/>

just over a million workers in Canada earn the minimum wage, the kind of increase recommended here would have a significant impact on the economy and on poverty reduction, and since the real value of today's minimum wage — that is, the amount that the minimum wage can purchase — is less than it was in the mid-1970s, increases in minimum wages would seem to be fully justified.[12]

The case for a living wage is the same as the case for a higher minimum wage. A living wage sets a higher standard than the minimum wage. As economist Iglika Ivanova describes it, "The living wage is calculated as the hourly rate at which a household can meet its basic needs, once government transfers have been added to a family's income (such as the Universal Child Care Benefit) and deductions have been subtracted (such as income taxes and Employment Insurance premiums)."[13] The CCPA's Trish Hennessey adds: "A living wage isn't extravagant. It doesn't allow families to save for retirement, to save for their children's education, or to service their debt. But it does reflect the cost of affording the basics of life."[14] It is based, in other words, on the simple proposition that in a wealthy country such as Canada, those who do the work ought to be paid enough that they do not live in poverty and can meet their basic needs.[15] Calgary's Living Wage Action Team estimates that a living wage in that city in 2012 would be $14.50 per hour without benefits, or $13.00 per hour with benefits.[16] A living wage in Regina in 2014 is $16.46 per hour and in Victoria, for 2013, it is $18.73 per hour.[17] In 2010, the City of New Westminster in B.C. passed a living wage policy, the first city in Canada to do so, and a growing number of non-governmental organizations are also adopting living wage policies, including Vancity, Canada's largest credit union, which announced in 2011 that all of its employees and service providers will be paid a wage at least equivalent to the living wage. Both the economy at large and individual employers benefit from a living wage policy, and employees working in a living wage organization are lifted out of poverty.

EDUCATION

If low-income people are to move into good jobs, educational outcomes will have to be improved. Improved educational outcomes are essential to getting a good job, as well as being essential in promoting engaged citizenship and democratic values. Again, we know some important things about how to do this. It is essential to think strategically about the role of education in combatting poverty and to think

It takes a village...
In Québec, all parents pay the same childcare rate of $7 per child per day. In other provinces childcare can be as much as $2000 per month ($100 per day). The Quebec government spends $2.2 billion per year on this program (nearly 2/3 of the $3.6 billion spent by all provinces and territories combined), about 0.7% of GDP on childcare. The OECD recommends 1% is the minimum for a good quality childcare system. [Started] in fall of 1997, the program also includes expanded childbirth leave, including 5 weeks exclusively for fathers, full-day kindergarten and after school care. Labour force participation rate of women, aged 25–44 years, went from the lowest in Canada (except for Atlantic provinces) to the highest in the country. The number of single parents on welfare was cut in half and after-tax income rose by 81%. Over a 16-year period the rate of child poverty was reduced by half.

Source: Erin Anderssen and Kim Mackrael, "A $7 Revolution," Globe and Mail, October 19, p. F1, F6–F7

about education in a "whole-life" fashion, that is, from pre-school to adult education and all stages in between. For our purposes here, I will focus very briefly on three aspects of education — early childhood education and care (ECEC), adult education and on-reserve First Nations education. Increased investments in each of these would have a very significant effect in reducing poverty and producing broad economic benefits for all Canadians.

Early Childhood Education and Care

The benefits of increased public investment in high quality early childhood education and care (ECEC) are many. Single mothers and children in low-income families are especially likely to benefit from improved access to ECEC. The costs of not investing in ECEC are the failure to reap those benefits and the resultant failure to have a positive impact on the problems of complex poverty.

Yet despite the many benefits of ECEC, and the high cost of not investing in ECEC, childcare continues to be expensive for parents, with fees "often higher than university tuition,"[18] and the number of subsidized childcare spaces in Canada does not come close to meeting the demand. "More than 70 percent of mothers of young children are in the paid labour force, but in 2010 (the most recent available data) there were regulated spaces in child care centres for only about 21 percent of children 0–5 years old."[19]

A good poverty reduction plan would include targets and timelines for the creation of many thousands of additional childcare spaces across Canada in order to meet the demand for them. The plan would ensure that high quality regulated childcare is available especially in low-income areas, where EDI scores (early development instrument scores, which measure children's readiness for school at age five) are the lowest. And the plan would include a commitment — with targets and timelines — to train people from marginalized groups for employment as childcare workers and to construct these centres.

Can we afford this? Martha Friendly and Susan Prentice reply:

> Yes, several times over. Yes, because investing in young children is a wise use of resources and can lead to better outcomes for many children, particularly those marginalized by poverty and at-risk of social exclusion. Yes, because ECEC is a green and labour-intensive industry that is a part of sustainable local economic development, including creating jobs for women. Most importantly, "Yes," because as a developed nation we have the wealth and obligation to act for children and families. Many would say that a twenty-first-century country cannot afford anything less.[20]

Adult Education

Adult education is not nearly as well studied as ECEC, but a recent study of Aboriginal adult education in Winnipeg's low-income inner city shows that the right kinds of adult education can be transformative, and this is the case at the level of the individual, their families and their low-income communities.[21] The lives of individual adult learners are transformed, in very positive ways. Families of adult learners are positively affected: "There is often a 'ripple effect,' as once the first person in a family takes the plunge into adult education, others in the family — often many others — soon follow, and children and grandchildren do better in school." And at the level of the community, many Aboriginal adult graduates choose to "give back" to their low-income communities: "Rather than leaving behind the communities from which they have come, many give back to those communities, contributing to making the broader socio-economic changes that are necessary to break the cycle by which poverty produces poor educational outcomes which then contribute to still more poverty."[22]

As is the case with ECEC, the economic benefits are substantial, as was shown above with the case of the Urban Circle Training Centre in Winnipeg's inner city, which saved taxpayers — by moving students from social assistance to reasonably well-paid jobs — an estimated $53.5 million.[23] If one relatively small adult education centre can produce these kinds of financial benefits, it follows that a widespread strategic approach to adult education for marginalized communities would be even more economically beneficial.

On-Reserve First Nations Education

We should also be investing at least as much per student in First Nations on-reserve schools as we do in the regular, non-Aboriginal school system. Right now, this is not the case. It has been estimated that Federal Government expenditures for on-reserve education for First Nations students are $2000–$3000 per student per year less than expenditures on students in the regular school system. This is a factor in the much lower high school graduation rates of on-reserve First Nations youth. As shown in Chapter 5, Sharpe et al. have estimated that investing in First Nations education would, over the twenty-five year period from 2001–26, increase Canada's economic output by $401 billion and Canada's tax revenues by $39 billion.[24]

It seems clear from the evidence that Canada should be investing much more than we now do in ECEC, adult education and First Nations education. These investments should be strategic, that is, investments should be made especially in educational initiatives that have proved to be effective and that disproportionately benefit those who are poor. Doing so will reduce poverty levels significantly, which will produce economic gains that accrue to the benefit of all Canadians.

THE UNION ADVANTAGE

Trade unions are a crucial part of a poverty reduction plan. It is well established that workers represented by a union enjoy higher wages and better benefits than workers who are not represented by a union.[25] This is called the "union advantage." The union advantage is greatest for those who might otherwise be poor — "workers with less formal education and skills, younger and less experienced workers, and women and workers of colour who experience discrimination in the job market" — with the result that unions have been able to "reduce the overall incidence of low pay and poverty."[26] For young workers aged 15–29 years, for example, those in a union earned $5.53 per hour *more* in 2012 than those not in a union,[27] a considerable advantage in light of the economic challenges facing young Canadians.

In addition, unions have long been leading organizations in the struggle for improved living conditions beyond the workplace, and this too contributes significantly to poverty reduction. As described by Errol Black and Jim Silver:

> The list of achievements is impressive: child labour laws, Workers' Compensation, Workplace Health and Safety legislation, minimum wage and employment standards legislation, government pension plans (the Old Age Pension, the Canada Pension Plan), Medicare, Home Care, and community development programs for municipalities.…
> All of these programs provide benefits that are accessible to all of us, irrespective of our socio-economic status.

In this way, trade unions have played an essential role in building a Canada that has been more egalitarian than it would have been in their absence. And the evidence is now overwhelming and irrefutable that a more egalitarian society is a healthier society — in every way.[28]

The role of governments and government legislation is crucial in enabling trade unions to exist and to engage in struggles to improve the lives of those who might otherwise be poor. Government legislation can make it easier, or harder, for workers who want to form unions and negotiate first collective agreements to do so. Under neoliberalism, governments in the U.S. and Canada have been making it increasingly difficult for workers to form unions and negotiate collective agreements, most recently introducing or planning to introduce what is misleadingly called "right to work" legislation, which enables members of unions to enjoy all the benefits their unions produce without having to pay union dues. This has the effect of severely weakening unions. As well as right to work laws, U.S. legislators have introduced hundreds of anti-union bills in recent years, while "Canada's federal and provincial governments have passed two hundred pieces of legislation since 1982 that have restricted, suspended, or denied collective bargaining rights for Canadian workers."[29] As a result, union density — the proportion of workers who are unionized — has declined in the U.S. to 12 percent overall and less than 7 percent in the private sector, and in the private sector in Canada it is down to one in six workers.[30]

This dramatic weakening of the trade union movement has been a deliberate part of the strategy of neoliberalism, undertaken precisely because unions are essential organizations in the battle against inequality and poverty and the struggle for a more shared prosperity.

As economist Andrew Jackson puts it: "It is no exaggeration to say that unions were the prime architects of the middle class and shared prosperity."[31] Harvard University's Garry Sran and his colleagues add:

> There is extensive research that suggests there are signifi-
> cant social benefits for countries with strong labour rights
> and a more extensive collective bargaining system. Income
> inequality is less extreme according to a variety of measures,
> civic engagement is higher, there are more extensive social
> programs such as health care and pension plans, and the
> incidence of poverty is significantly smaller.[32]

This is why unions are now under attack by neoliberal governments and organizations. As the Director of Americans for Prosperity, a right-wing, neoliberal organization in the U.S. said: "What we would like to see is to take the unions out at the knees so that they don't have the resources to fight these battles"[33] — that is, the battles against inequality and poverty. As union strength has been eroded, inequality has grown; high levels of inequality produce many societal disadvantages — poorer health, lower levels of educational attainment and higher incidences of crime, for example. There is clear evidence that the lower the rate of unionization in a country, the greater will be the degree of inequality. Trade union researcher Chris Schenk observes that "the two countries with the largest declines in unionization are the United States and the United Kingdom." As Schenk says, "These two countries have also experienced the largest increase in wage inequality," which in turn contributes to "issues of weakened health, inadequate housing, poor diet, less readiness to learn, higher levels of mental illness and crime, reduced productivity and indeed, lifespan," all of which are the central features of complex poverty.[34] Similarly,

Juha Mikkonen and Dennis Raphael, social determinants of health researchers, show that the lower a country's union density, the higher is the rate of child poverty. They argue that the most important step in improving the social determinants of health and thus combatting inequality and poverty "is making it easier for Canadians to unionize their workplace."[35] It is clear that a strong and healthy trade union movement is a crucial part of an effective poverty reduction plan.

HOUSING

There is a crisis in Canada's low-income rental housing market, with demand for such housing far outstripping supply.[36] The result is low vacancy rates, high and rising rental costs and many low-income families and individuals living in housing that is not affordable, and/or not large enough, and/or in poor condition. The problem is worsened by the fact that social assistance rates and wages at the low end of the income scale, including minimum wages, are so low that many families do not have enough left for food after paying so much of their limited income on rent. The result can be inadequate diets, with adverse health implications, or frequent moves in search of better housing, with adverse effects on children's schooling. In these and other ways — for example, housing that is poorly insulated and cold in winter and/or housing that is infested with bedbugs or rodents — housing becomes an important social determinant of health and can play an important role in perpetuating complex poverty.

A major part of the problem with low-income rental housing is the fact that 95 percent of Canada's housing is built by private, for-profit developers. Generally speaking, they do not build new, low-income rental housing, because there is little or no profit to be made in doing so, and there is little or no profit to be made because the incomes of those in need of such rental housing — and thus the rents that they can pay — are so low. The housing that gets built is that which will earn a profit — large, detached suburban homes and expensive condos, for example. Low-income rental does not get built, and much that was previously built is now being turned into condos. Thus low-income rental housing is in short supply, and often that which does exist is in poor condition, at least in part because the rents that poor people can afford are not high enough to make it financially viable for landlords to make needed repairs.

The solution requires that governments play a much-expanded role in the provision of "social housing" — that is, housing that is subsidized. Canada's Federal Government largely abandoned social housing in 1993, resulting in a dramatic decline in social housing. The housing problem facing poor people has grown steadily worse ever since.

Canada needs a national housing strategy — we are the only major industrial country in the world without one.[37] A good national housing strategy would include a dramatic increase in the supply of subsidized, low-income rental housing. Because housing is such an important social determinant of health and is so foundational in enabling people to become stabilized enough to take advantage of educational and employment opportunities, the availability of good quality, affordable housing — social housing — will in itself significantly improve the lives of low-income people. Good quality housing that is affordable for low-income people is a central aspect of neighbourhood renewal in low-income areas because it stabilizes families, and stable families can become the building blocks of healthy individuals and communities. And in addition, the increased production of social housing units will create large numbers of jobs, and good jobs are needed to pull people out of poverty. The poverty reduction character of a national housing strategy could be further improved if it were linked to a deliberate strategy of training and hiring those living in poverty so that the new jobs would be filled by people otherwise marginalized from the paid labour force.

Financing a national housing strategy would have to be carefully considered, because housing is expensive. However, as the Canadian Centre for Policy Alternatives' Alternative Federal Budget 2013 points out, the large revenues being generated by Canada Mortgage and Housing Corporation (CMHC) could be used to fund housing, and/or "a new Government of Canada–backed bond (perhaps tax-exempt) could finance a national affordable housing trust to pay for new housing supply and repairs to existing housing."[38] Similarly, the tax revenues generated in ways suggested below could also be applied, in part, to a national housing strategy.

COMMUNITY ECONOMIC DEVELOPMENT

In low-income communities struggling with complex poverty, community economic development (CED) can be an important part of an effective poverty reduction plan. Good CED requires the active participation of, and takes its direction from, members of the low-income communities in which it is being practised because poor people have crucial experiential knowledge of their community's needs and strengths that outsiders are not likely to have. The best CED is asset-based, which means that it identifies strengths in a low-income community — even the most challenged communities have many strengths — and builds on those strengths. And the best CED uses a "convergence approach," which is characterized by training and employing local people, purchasing locally, investing locally and producing to meet local peoples' needs.[39] An example of a convergence approach is a housing strategy that builds rental housing for

BUILDing healthy families and strong communities

Building Urban Industries for Local Development (BUILD) – is a social enterprise non-profit contractor and a training program for people who face barriers to employment. BUILD retrofits homes with insulation and high-efficiency toilets as well as water-and-energy-saving devices (showerheads, CFLs, etc).

BUILD aims to support the local economy. For example, they purchase materials from Pollock's Hardware Co-op, a North End consumer cooperative. At company functions, and as part of their lunch program, they shop at Neechi Foods Community Store, a workers' cooperative. They partner and keep in touch with many North End and Aboriginal organizations, and encourage all of their employees to get involved in their communities.

Many BUILD employees are survivors (or the children of survivors) of the residential school system, the "60s scoop," gang life, or the foster care and criminal justice systems. BUILD programs aim to help employees' journeys towards healing. And, its training and apprenticeship positions provide much-needed employment.

BUILD also provides social and cultural programs—from classes on parenting to workshops on money-management—for its employees. Healthier families reduce health care and employment income assistance, as well as criminal justice costs. Healthy families means having food on the table, having a good place to live and having a stable home life. A pay-cheque can provide some, but not all, of these healthy family requirements.

Source: SEC <http://socialenterprisecentrewpg.org/friends-partners/build-inc/> and BUILD <http://buildinc.ca/>

low-income people because that is the kind of housing that is most needed, trains and hires local low-income people to do the building because they need the jobs, purchases building supplies from local suppliers who also hire and train low-income people, and invests any surplus that may be earned back into the low-income community to continue to meet people's needs.

Winnipeg's inner city is an example of a very low-income community that is home to a great deal of effective CED activity, much of which uses a convergence approach. The Social Enterprise Centre, for example, houses a number of effective community-based organizations, including BUILD and Manitoba Green Retrofit, both of which train local people — most of whom are very marginalized from the dominant economy and Aboriginal, while some are ex-street gang members — to retrofit inner-city buildings and provide other needed services, including, for example, bed bug remediation.

Many "alternative" educational institutions have emerged in the inner city, and they have developed strategies that are highly effective in enabling low-income and marginalized people living in complex poverty to improve their educational skills. A particularly important aspect of this education is that a high proportion of graduates choose to give back to the communities in which they have been raised by using their educational credentials and their experiential knowledge to work for positive change in those communities in a fashion that is consistent with a convergence approach.[40] Neighbourhood renewal corporations have emerged in most Winnipeg inner-city neighbourhoods, and they serve to identify, promote and coordinate community-building activities and to engage neighbourhood residents in this work.[41] Community-based Aboriginal organizations are especially effective in meeting the needs of marginalized urban Aboriginal people and have developed their own unique, decolonization-oriented approaches to CED.[42] Winnipeg's inner city has a particularly rich array of effective community-based organizations that make use of a convergence approach to CED.

All of these activities are characterized by, in addition to the features described above, the two-sided process by which members of low-income communities, supported by their community-based organizations, identify problems and potential solutions, and governments — in the case of Winnipeg's inner city, primarily the provincial NDP government — invest in these solutions. This community-government collaboration can be very effective. A good example is Lord Selkirk Park (LSP), a large, 314-unit public housing project in the heart

"This is Turtle Island. This is where kids go after school to keep some of them out of trouble. They have a basketball court. There is a program there where young people can help clean up the neighbourhood. It's close to David Livingstone School." — Photo and caption by an inner-city youth.

Source: *CCPA-MB, 2013,* A Youth Lens on Poverty in Winnipeg: State of the Inner City Report 2013, *Winnipeg, p. 35*

of Winnipeg's North End. For decades, LSP was considered to be one of the worst neighbourhoods in the inner city, and in the 1990s it was only half-occupied, with many of the units boarded up and residents and social service workers referring to it as a "war zone." Beginning in 2005, the North End Community Renewal Corporation coordinated a CED strategy, to which the provincial government made significant public investments in strategies identified by the community. The strategy has produced a remarkable turnaround in the community. LSP is now fully occupied, with lower turnover than ever before and, for the first time in recent decades, a wait list of people who want to get in. LSP has become, as the result of the kind of CED strategy described here, a good place to live.[43]Almost every aspect of a good poverty reduction plan would benefit from the application of a CED approach. To take but one example, a national childcare strategy would build childcare centres across the country, targeting low-income communities in particular; hire from communities most marginalized from the paid labour force to construct the new childcare centres; train people from marginalized communities to become childcare workers, and in particular develop strategies to train and hire culturally appropriate childcare workers; and purchase supplies for childcare centres — food for snacks for example — from local food providers that themselves employ people from marginalized communities.

SOCIAL ASSISTANCE

If all the measures identified above were put in place, the numbers of people living in poverty, and the numbers on social assistance, would be dramatically reduced. However, there will always be some people in need of our support, in need of social assistance, and the rates and requirements of social assistance programs should be such that recipients can live in dignity.

That is often not the case today. During the neoliberal era of the last thirty-plus years, almost all forms of social assistance have been seriously eroded. The National Council of Welfare identifies the characteristics of social assistance in Canada today: "Requirements to be nearly destitute to qualify ... and complex rules and restrictions that are highly intrusive and make it hard to get ahead."[44] That this is so is completely consistent with the ideology of neoliberalism, which calls

Social assistance works

Bolsa Familia (the "Family Grant"), a Brazilian social program, basically, hands out cash to poor families, very poor families by Canadian standards. The program cost $11.5 billion in 2013, 0.46% of Brazil's GDP.

Bolsa Familia grants have two strings tied to them: (1) children in recipient families have to go to public health centres for regular checkups and the children have to be in school until they finish high school; (2) the grant goes into a bank account of the designated woman of the family who is given a debit card to use the money. It is guaranteed to the families – gives them certainty, the ability to plan their finances (a regular income to budget with). 75 percent of adult recipients work, 50 percent of total recipients do not because they are under 14 years old.

Between 2003, when it started, and 2009, incomes of the poorest grew at 7 times the rate of incomes of the richest Brazilians. Infant mortality decreased by 40 percent and school enrolment for the poor sits at 100 percent — children in *Bolsa* families graduate at twice the rate of non-*Bolsa* families.

Teresa Campello, Minister of Social Development: "This thing about being suspicious — oh, you have to supervise poor people because they will spend it wrong – that is just not true."

Source: Stephanie Nolan, 2013, "What Would Robin Hood Do?" Globe and Mail, December 28, p. F1, F6

for reductions in government spending, extols the virtues of small government, places a high value on individualism and is inclined to blame the poor for their plight. President Ronald Reagan, who was elected in 1980 and played a key role in bringing neoliberalism to the U.S., promoted his attack on social assistance by referring disparagingly to "welfare queens" — African-American single mothers who purportedly abused the system by having children simply to draw additional social assistance benefits.[45] This was a crude and dishonest stereotype that drew, deliberately and, in important respects, successfully, on the long history of racism in the U.S. in order to generate resentment against social assistance recipients and earn public support for the cuts that soon followed.

Yet in the Canadian case, the 1974–9 mincome experiment — that is, a minimum income (mincome) or guaranteed annual income beneath which nobody could fall — in Dauphin, Manitoba, suggests that placing a reasonable floor under all Canadians does not lead to abuse of the system or to reduced levels of employment. This has been shown in studies of mincome done years later by economist Evelyn Forget.[46] On the contrary, mincome produced many positive outcomes, including the fact that a higher proportion of students continued on to grade 12, the incidence of hospitalization was reduced and visits to doctors for mental health issues were also reduced. Hours of paid employment went down, but this was almost exclusively because mothers of young children delayed returning to the work force to spend more time with their children, and young people continued in school rather than leaving school prior to graduation in order to work. The results of this guaranteed annual income experiment appear to have been entirely positive. My own personal experience of working in Winnipeg's low-income inner city in various ways for almost twenty years is that many poor people quickly become tired of being on welfare and come to fear and dislike their "worker" — the social worker who monitors and manages their "case" — and they respond positively to well-designed and properly supported opportunities that hold out the promise of their being able to improve their circumstances in ways and to ends of their choosing.

Oscar Lewis and the "culture of poverty"[47] are wrong, at least insofar as arguing that people living in complex poverty adapt to it and become unable/unwilling to respond to opportunities for change. This is likely to be true only in the short term, and only in the case of some people who have been particularly badly damaged by their experience of complex poverty. William Julius Wilson was right in arguing that while people do adapt to complex poverty and do develop cultural attributes like those described by Lewis, they need not be trapped.[48] Change their economic and social opportunities, and in most cases people will seize those opportunities. What necessarily follows is that a poverty reduction plan should create *opportunities* for poor people, and in particular the kinds of opportunities that poor people themselves say they want; *tailor* those opportunities to the particular circumstances of the people at whom they are directed; provide *supports* to enable people to take advantage of those tailored opportunities; and create "*laddered*" opportunities, so that poor people hitherto mired in the web of complex poverty can move forward in a step-by-step fashion as the circumstances of their lives allow.[49] When this is done and the other measures described above — job creation, education, housing, for example — are implemented, most people who are able to do so will respond positively and will change their lives in ways that are beneficial to themselves, to their families and to the community. The remainder, almost all of whom are unable, for various reasons, to take advantage of these opportunities, should still be able to live in dignity. Social assistance programs should be designed accordingly — doing so is an essential part of a poverty reduction strategy.

WHERE DOES THE MONEY COME FROM?

How is a poverty reduction plan like the one outlined here to be paid for? A part of the answer is that it will pay for itself, as shown in Chapter 5. Poverty costs Canadians many billions of dollars annually; reducing poverty saves a large portion of those costs. The difficulty is that the investment needed to effect a large reduction in poverty needs to be made now; the benefits in terms of savings will only be realized in future. In many cases, the benefits will begin to appear in a matter of years; in others, the full benefits may take a generation or more. Where are the admittedly large sums of money needed for the up-front investment to come from initially? The answer is, in part, from changes to the tax system.

After thirty years of neoliberalism, Canadians have been led to believe that taxes are a bad thing. Neoliberal governments and right-wing think tanks such as the Fraser Institute and the C.D. Howe Institute have spent years persuading Canadians that taxes are a "burden," and most of the media have joined them in what has become, for many Canadians, a self-evident truth. But it is not true. Far from being a bad thing, taxes are the price we pay for a civilized society.

Citizens of the Nordic countries, for example, enjoy among the highest standards of living in the world. Their relatively egalitarian economies produce societies that are healthy in every respect and produce far lower levels of poverty than is the case in Canada. The price they pay is higher rates of taxation. This enables them to take a "solidarity" approach to governance — citizens of these countries are in solidarity with their fellow citizens; they share a collective responsibility, a moral obligation, for each other, and this is achieved through a redistributive state funded by levels of taxation higher than is the case in Canada. This is the opposite, in important respects, of the neoliberal approach with its commitment to individualism, which leaves people to a much greater extent to their own devices, with the result that some become exceptionally wealthy while many become poor, and far too many become very poor.

Are there ways for Canada to increase its tax revenues in order to be able to implement an effective poverty reduction plan? The answer, many Canadians believe, is yes. Even representatives of organizations that have until recently led the struggle for lower taxes, particularly on corporations and high income individuals, are beginning to rethink their positions in the face of the many needs confronting our country. For example, Don Drummond, former chief economist of the TD Bank and co-chair of the C.D. Howe's Fiscal and Tax Competitiveness Council, told the *Globe and Mail* that we Canadians need to change our cultural views about taxation and that the Nordic countries offer a good example to emulate: "If you stand back in the abstract and shop around the world for what kind of economic or taxation model you might want to emulate, you really have to pause and take note of what's happening in northern Europe."[50] One aspect of a reformulated taxation strategy for Canada would have to be higher rates of taxation on the wealthiest Canadians and on corporations. It is they who have, in recent years, derived enormous benefits from the tax cuts that are the product of thirty years of neoliberalism. It is social spending that has suffered in relative terms:

> The share of the GDP that Canada devotes to social spending has dropped steadily and when last measured stood at just 16 percent, a dismal 22nd out of 30 OECD (Organization

for Economic Cooperation and Development) nations. The average OECD nation spends about 23 percent of GDP on its social programs, and some countries, such as Sweden and France, spend as much as 27 percent.[51]

This reduction in the share of our GDP that goes to social spending is in large part a function of recent tax cuts; Canada could increase its social spending — and in particular could introduce a strong poverty reduction plan — by reversing recent tax cuts. Economist Jim Stanford refers to data produced by the OECD that show that since 2000, Canada has reduced its tax revenues by a larger proportion than any other major industrial country and the result has been "foregone revenue of more than $100 billion."[52] And there appears to be public support for reversing these tax cuts. Stanford observes, "Polls have put public support for some new taxes — especially those targeted at corporations and the wealthy — near 80 percent."[53]

The traditional argument is that higher taxes on the wealthy and on corporations will scare them away, with the result that Canada would lose the advantage of the investments that wealthy individuals and corporations would otherwise have made, and governments would take in even less revenue as a consequence. In other words, this argument is that tax cuts on the wealthy and on corporations are counterproductive. Yet the broad evidence does not seem to support what is really just a hypothesis. Paul Krugman, recipient of the prestigious Nobel Prize for Economics, observes: "Researchers have studied the revenue effects of tax hikes (and cuts) about as thoroughly as any topic in economics, and the evidence is decisive: increasing top tax rates from their current level would lead to substantially higher revenue."[54] And Joseph Stiglitz, also a recipient of the Nobel Prize for Economics, former chief economist of the World Bank and former chair of the Council of Economic Advisors, the economic advisory body to the U.S. President, said: "We have an unmanageable, unfair, distortionary global tax regime" that is creating dangerously growing levels of inequality as well as "the starving of the public sector which has been pivotal in America no longer being the land of opportunity."[55] Canada, like other advanced industrial countries that have been following the neoliberal approach of tax cuts, needs to raise taxes. As Iglika Ivanova and Seth Klein have put it: "There is a clear need to raise more tax revenues. There is considerable room to do so. And the options for doing so are many."[56]

This is not the appropriate place to go into detail about tax policy. However, the principles of a fairer and more economically healthy tax policy ought to include the fact that taxes are a good thing and that taxes should be imposed in a way that is progressive — that is, the more a person or corporation earns, the higher is the proportion of their income that they pay in taxes. These principles might find expression in the following progressive tax changes: reversing the previous cuts to marginal tax rates on very high income earners; reversing the previous cuts to corporate tax rates; reversing the two percentage point cut to the Goods and Services Tax (GST); introducing an inheritance tax— "Canada is currently one of the few developed countries that does not tax bequests or inheritances"[57]; and rationalizing "tax expenditures," the various deductions and tax credits available to wealthy individuals and corporations. These and other revenue-generating tax changes can be done in a way that is fair and is seen to be fair. These tax changes would be likely to find broad public support, and they would generate the public funds needed to implement an effective poverty reduction plan.

CHANGE REQUIRES EFFORT

None of these things — significantly increased public investment in the various elements of the kind of poverty reduction plan described in this chapter, increased levels of taxation on those most able to pay in order to cover the costs of these investments — is going to happen without a struggle. Higher levels of public investment and taxation are contrary to the dominant ideology of our times — neoliberalism. Therefore, if there is to be a concerted attack on poverty in Canada, we cannot simply wait for governments — those that exist today and those that will succeed them — to do it. We have to demand that they do it. This requires that people — including small groups of people in various parts of the country — organize themselves and develop effective campaigns demanding that governments act purposefully and strongly to make dramatic reductions in the level of poverty. Great advances in human betterment are made because people demand that such advances be made. A massive reduction in the level of poverty in Canada would be just such a great advance. And as Tommy Douglas, the Canadian most responsible for the creation of medicare, put it: "Courage my friends; 'tis not too late to build a better world."

A better world, or at least a better Canada, is one in which the poverty that so many Canadians currently endure is dramatically reduced to a fraction of its current level. Doing so is possible; doing so is beneficial; and doing so will require that we Canadians organize ourselves to make demands upon governments that will force them to invest in poverty reduction solutions.

NOTES

Chapter 1: Forms of Poverty

1.   Thomas Berger, 1991, *A Long and Terrible Shadow: White Values, Native Rights in the Americas, 1492–1992,* Vancouver and Toronto: Douglas and McIntyre.

2.   Jim Silver, 2011, *Good Places to Live: Poverty and Public Housing in Canada,* Halifax: Fernwood Publishing.

3.   National Council of Welfare (NCW), 2011, *The Dollars and Sense of Solving Poverty,* Ottawa: National Council of Welfare, p. 79.

Chapter 2: Poverty by the Numbers

1.   Statistics Canada, 2010, *Market Basket Measure (2008 base)* <www.statcan.gc.ca/pub/75f0002m/2010005/mbm-mpc-eng.htm> accessed August 10, 2013.

2.   Statistics Canada, 2012, *Low-Income in Canada: A Multi-Line and Multi-Index Perspective,* Catalogue no. 75F0002M, no. 001, Ottawa.

3.   Rob Valletta, 2005, *The Ins and Outs of Poverty in Advanced Economies: Poverty Dynamics in Canada, Germany, Great Britain and the United States,* Catalogue no. 75F0002M1E-No. 001, Ottawa: Statistics Canada, p. 12.

4.   Raphael, Dennis. 2009. "Poverty, Human Development and Health in Canada: Research, Practice and Advocacy Dilemmas." *Canadian Journal of Nursing Research,* 41, 2.

5.   Juha Mikkonen and Dennis Raphael, 2010, *Social Determinants of*

Health: The Canadian Facts, Toronto: York University School of Health Policy and Management, p. 25.

6. National Council of Welfare (NCW), 2004, *Poverty Profile 2001,* Ottawa, pp. 107–10.

7. Monica Townson, 2009, *Women's Poverty and the Recession,* Ottawa: Canadian Centre for Policy Alternatives, p. 16.

8. Ontario Common Front (OCF), 2012, *Falling Behind: Ontario's Backslide into Widening Inequality, Growing Poverty and Cuts to Social Programs,* Toronto, p. 19.

9. Mary Cornish, 2012, *A Living Wage as a Human Right,* Toronto: Canadian Centre for Policy Alternatives-Ontario, pp. 7–8; Mary Cornish, 2013, *Ten Ways to Close Ontario's Gender Pay Gap,* Toronto: Canadian Centre for Policy Alternatives-Ontario, p. 6.

10. Pat Armstrong, 2008, "Equal Pay for Work of Equal Value," Expert Report prepared for the Public Service Alliance of Canada in the Federal Court of Canada proceeding, *Public Service Alliance of Canada and Nicole Turmel v. Her Majesty the Queen in Right of Canada,* Court File No. T-1949-00, p. 1.

11. National Council of Welfare, 2001, *Poverty Profile 1998,* Ottawa.

12. Karen Foster, 2012, *Youth Employment and Un(der) Employment,* Ottawa: Canadian Centre for Policy Alternatives, p. 4.

13. Benjamin Tal, 2013, *Dimensions of Youth Unemployment in Canada* Toronto: CIBC World Markets Inc., p. 13.

14. Armine Yalnizyan, 1998, *The Growing Gap: A Report on Growing Inequality between Rich and Poor in Canada,* Toronto: Centre for Social Justice, p. 24.

15. Rob Carrick, 2013, "The Scary Decline of Housing Affordability," *Globe and Mail,* June 18.

16. Ontario Common Front (OCF), 2012, *Falling Behind: Ontario's Backslide into Widening Inequality, Growing Poverty and Cuts to Social Programs,* Toronto.

17. David Macdonald and Erika Shaker, 2012, *Eduflation and the High Cost of Learning,* Ottawa: Canadian Centre for Policy Alternatives; Statistics Canada, 2012, *Table 202-0603, Average after-tax income, by economic*

family type, 2011 constant dollars, annual (dollars), CANSIM (database).

18. Quoted in *Winnipeg Free Press*, 2013, "Youth Still Face Gloom; Issue Gets Political," May 11.

19. Grace-Edward Galabuzi, 2006, *Canada's Economic Apartheid: The Social Exclusion of Racialized Groups in the New Century,* Toronto: Canadian Scholars' Press, p. 183, 186.

20. Sheila Block and Grace-Edward Galabuzi, 2011, *Canada's Colour Coded Labour Market,* Ottawa and Toronto: Canadian Centre for Policy Alternatives and the Wellesley Institute, p. 5.

21. Ibid, p. 7.

22. OCF, *Falling Behind,* p. 24, 6.

23. Sheila Block and Grace-Edward Galabuzi, p. 4.

24. Darren Lezubski, Jim Silver and Errol Black, 2000, "High and Rising: The Growth of Poverty in Winnipeg," in Jim Silver (ed.), *Solutions that Work: Fighting Poverty in Winnipeg,* Halifax: Fernwood Publishing.

25. Statistics Canada, customized data, Social Planning Council of Winnipeg 2001.

26. Daniel Wilson and David McDonald, 2010, *The Income Gap Between Aboriginal Peoples and the Rest of Canada,* Ottawa: Canadian Centre for Policy Alternatives, p. 8.

27. David Macdonald and Daniel Wilson, 2013, *Poverty or Prosperity: Indigenous Children in Canada,* Ottawa: Canadian Centre for Policy Alternatives.

28. Ibid, p. 5.

29. Food Banks Canada, 2013, *Hunger Count: A Comprehensive Report on Hunger and Food Bank Use in Canada, and Recommendations for Change,* Toronto.

30. Food Banks Canada, 2012, *Hunger Count: A Comprehensive Report on Hunger and Food Bank Use in Canada, and Recommendations for Change,* Toronto, p. 2.

31. Ken Battle, 1996, *Precarious Labour Market Fuels Rising Poverty,* Ottawa: Caledon Institute.

32. John Stapleton, Brian Murphy and Yue Xing, 2012, *The 'Working Poor' in the Toronto Region: Who They Are, Where They Live, and How Trends*

Are Changing, Toronto: Metcalf Foundation, p. 24–25.

33. Canada, 2012, *The National Child Benefit Progress Report 2008,* Ottawa: Public Works and Government Services, p. 28.

34. Statistics Canada, 2009, *Labour Force Historical Review 2009,* Table 002, Catalogue No. 71F0004XVB.

35. Grace-Edward Galabuzi, 2006, p. xii, 125.

36. Grant Schellenberg, 1997, *The Changing Nature of Part-Time Work,* Ottawa: Canadian Council on Social Development, p. 39.

37. Statistics Canada, 2006, *Canada's Changing Labour Force, 2006 Census,* Ottawa.

38. Benjamin Tal, 2013, p. 4.

39. Grant Schellenberg, 1997, p. 2.

40. Dominique Fleury and Myriam Fortin, 2006, *When Working Is Not Enough to Escape Poverty: An Analysis of Canada's Working Poor,* Ottawa: Human Resources and Social Development Canada, p. ii.

41. Ken Battle, 1999, *Poverty Eases Slightly,* Ottawa: Caledon Institute, p. 4.

42. Ken Battle, 2011, *Restoring Minimum Wages in Canada,* Ottawa: Caledon Institute, p. 44.

43. Dennis Raphael, 2009, "Poverty, Human Development and Health in Canada: Research, Practice and Advocacy Dilemmas," *Canadian Journal of Nursing Research* 41, 2, p. 8.

44. Conference Board of Canada, 2013, *How Canada Performs: A Report Card on Canada,* Ottawa. <www.conferenceboard.ca/hcp/details/society/child-poverty.aspx> accessed August 8, 2013.

45. National Council of Welfare (NCW), 1996, *Poverty Profile 1994,* Ottawa: Minister of Supply and Services, p. 13.

46. David Ross and Paul Roberts, 1999, *Income and Child Well-Being: A New Perspective on the Poverty Debate,* Ottawa: Canadian Council on Social Development, p. 3.

47. David Ross and Paul Roberts, 1999, p. 8, 25, 34, 36.

48. Canadian Council on Social Development (CCSD), 1994, *Countdown '94: Campaign 2000 Child Poverty Indicator Report,* Ottawa, p. 1.

49. National Council of Welfare (NCW), 1975, *Poor Kids: A Report by the*

National Council of Welfare on Children in Poverty in Canada, Ottawa, p. 1.

50. Marni Brownell, Randy Fransoo and Patricia Martens, 2010, "Social Determinants of Health and the Distribution of Health Outcomes in Manitoba," in Lynne Fernandez, Shauna MacKinnon and Jim Silver (eds.), *The Social Determinants of Health in Manitoba,* Winnipeg: Canadian Centre for Policy Alternatives-Manitoba.

51. Elizabeth Comack, 2012, *Racialized Policing: Aboriginal People's Encounters with the Police,* Halifax and Winnipeg: Fernwood Publishing, p. 84.

52. Jim Silver, 2010, "Segregated City: A Century of Poverty in Winnipeg," in Paul Thomas and Curtis Brown (eds.), *Manitoba Politics and Government: Issues, Institutions, Traditions,* Winnipeg: University of Manitoba Press.

53. Armine Yalnizyan, 2013, "Boost the Minimum Wage, Boost the Economy," *Progressive Economics Forum,* February 27. <www.progressive-economics.ca/2013/02/27/boost-the-minimum> p. 3.

54. Armine Yalnizyan, 2007, *The Rich and the Rest of Us: The Changing Face of Canada's Growing Gap,* Ottawa: Canadian Centre for Policy Alternatives, p. 28.

55. Hugh Mackenzie, 2013, *All in a Day's Work? CEO Pay in Canada,* Ottawa: Canadian Centre for Policy Alternatives, p. 3–4.

56. Armine Yalnizyan, 2010, *The Rise of Canada's Richest 1 Percent,* Ottawa: Canadian Centre for Policy Alternatives, p. 21.

57. Lars Osberg, 2008, *A Quarter Century of Economic Inequality in Canada: 1981–2006,* Ottawa: Canadian Centre for Policy Alternatives, p. 23.

58. Armine Yalnizyan, 2007, p. 3–4.

59. Jordan Brennan, 2012, *A Shrinking Universe: How Concentrated Corporate Power Is Shaping Income Inequality in Canada,* Ottawa: Canadian Centre for Policy Alternatives, p. 34.

60. Jim Stanford, 2011, "Canada's Billionaires," *The Monitor,* Ottawa: Canadian Centre for Policy Alternatives, November, p. 2.

61. Barbara Garson, 2013, "How the 40-Year 'Long Recession' Led to the Great Recession," *TomDispatch,* April 9.

62. Emmanuel Saez, 2013, *Striking It Richer: The Evolution of Top Incomes in the United States (Updated with 2011 Estimates).*<elsa.berkeley.edu/~Saez/Saez-USstopincomes-2011.pdf> p. 2.

63. Dave Zweifel, 2010, "There Is Class War, and Rich Are Winning," October 6. <www.commondreams.org/headline/2010/10/06-5> accessed August 15, 2013.

64. Armine Yalnizyan, 2007, p. 9, 15.

Chapter 3: Neoliberalism and Its Effects

1. Neil Smith, 2012, *After Neoliberalism.* Annual Lecture, Cities Group, King's College, London, March 12, p. 1.

2. Gary Teeple, 2000, *Globalization and the Decline of Social Reform into the 21st Century, First Edition,* Toronto: Garamond Press, p. 91.

3. Ibid, p. 67.

4. Quoted in Tavia Grant, 2013, "Employers' boon, Canada's not so much," *Globe and Mail Report on Business,* April 20, p. B4.

5. Jim Stanford, 2013, "It'll Take More Than Window-Dressing to Fix This Problem," *CCPA Monitor,* June.

6. Thom Hartmann and Sam Sacks, 2012, "America the Third-World Nation in Just 4 Easy Steps," *The Daily Take, Op-Ed,* November 10.

7. International Monetary Fund (IMF), 2013, *Canada: 2012 Article IV Consultation,* Washington, D.C.: International Monetary, p. 42.

8. Food Banks Canada, 2013, *Hunger Count: A Comprehensive Report on Hunger and Food Bank Use in Canada, and Recommendations for Change,* Toronto, p. 10.

9. Errol Black and Jim Silver, 2008, *Building a Better World: An Introduction to Trade Unionism in Canada, Second Edition,* Halifax and Winnipeg: Fernwood Publishing.

10. Chris Schenk, 2012, *Unions in a Democratic Society: A Response to the Consultation Paper on the Renewal of Labour Legislation in Saskatchewan,* Ottawa: Canadian Centre for Policy Alternatives.

11. Jordan Brennan, 2012, *A Shrinking Universe: How Concentrated Corporate Power Is Shaping Income Inequality in Canada,* Ottawa: Canadian Centre for Policy Alternatives, p. 17.

12. Robert Reich, 2013, "The Non Zero-Sum Society," *The Huffington Post*, August 18.

13. David McNally, 2009, "Inequality, the Profit System and Global Crisis," in Julie Guard and Wayne Antony (eds.), *Bankruptcies and Bailouts*, Halifax: Fernwood Publishing, p. 33, 43.

14. Eric Reguly, 2013, "Europe's Smouldering Fuse," *Globe and Mail Report on Business*, June 8.

15. Eric Reguly, 2013, "Europe's job destruction moves upstream," *Globe and Mail Report on Business*, May 1.

16. Michel Crozier, Samuel P. Huntington and Joji Watanuki, 1975, *The Crisis of Democracy: Report on the Governability of Democracies to the Trilateral Commission*, New York: New York University Press.

17. Armine Yalnizyan, 1998, *The Growing Gap: A Report on Growing Inequality between Rich and Poor in Canada*, Toronto: Centre for Social Justice, p. 64.

18. Jim Stanford, 2011, *Having Their Cake and Eating It Too: Business Profits, Taxes, and Investment in Canada*, Ottawa: Canadian Centre for Policy Alternatives, p. 11.

19. Armine Yalnizyan, 2010, *The Rise of Canada's Richest 1 Percent*, Ottawa: Canadian Centre for Policy Alternatives, p. 16.

20. Ibid, p. 17.

21. James S. Henry, 2012, *The Price of Offshore Revisited: New Estimates for "Missing" Global Private Wealth, Income Inequality, and Lost Taxes*, City: Tax Justice Network, p. 25.

22. Jim Stanford, 2011, Having Their Cake … .; Erin Weir, 2010, *Corporate Taxes and Investment in Ontario*, Ottawa: Canadian Centre for Policy Alternatives.

23. Gerald Friedman, 2013, "The Great Tax-Cut Experiment," *Dollars and Sense*, January/February.

24. Jane Pulkingham and Gordon Ternowetsky, 1999, "Neoliberalism and Retrenchment: Employment, Universality, Safety Net Provisions and a Collapsing Canadian Welfare State," in Dave Broad and Wayne Antony (eds.), *Citizens or Consumers? Social Policy in a Market Society*, Halifax: Fernwood Publishing, p. 93; Armine Yalnizyan, 1998, p. 56.

25. Jane Pulkingham and Gordon Ternowetsky 1999, p. 94.

26. Canadian Council on Social Development (CCSD), 1996, *Maintaining a National Social Safety Net: Recommendations on the Canada Health and Social Transfer*, Ottawa.

27. Armine Yalnizyan 1998, p. 57.

28. Stephen Gaetz, Jesse Donaldson, Tim Richter and Tanya Gulliver, 2013, *The State of Homelessness in Canada 2013*, Toronto: Canadian Homelessness Research Network Press, p. 15.

29. Quoted in Lars Osberg, 2008, *A Quarter Century of Economic Inequality in Canada: 1981–2006*, Ottawa: Canadian Centre for Policy Alternatives, p. 31–32.

30. Peter Edelman, 2012, *So Rich, So Poor: Why It's So Hard to End Poverty in America*, New York: The New Press.

31. Jason DeParle, 2012, "Welfare Limits Left Poor Adrift as Recession Hit," *New York Times*, April 7.

32. Jane Pulkingham and Gordon Ternowetsky, 1999, p. 86.

33. Canadian Labour Congress (CLC), 2003, *Falling Unemployment Insurance Protection for Canada's Unemployed*, Ottawa: Canadian Labour Congress.

34. Armine Yalnizyan, 2010, p. 20.

35. Julie Guard, 2012, "Conservatives' EI Reform Is a Bad-Jobs Policy," *Canadian Dimension* 46, 4 (July–August), p. 16–17.

36. Richard Shillington, 2008, *Evidence Provided to the Proceedings of the Sub Committee on Cities of the Standing Senate Committee on Social Affairs, Science and Technology*, May 29.

37. Gloria Galloway, 2013, "Conservatives load up Social Security Tribunal with allies," *Globe and Mail*, May 26.

38. Jim Stanford, 1996, "Discipline, Insecurity and Productivity: The Economics Behind Labour Market Productivity," in Jane Pulkingham and Gordon Ternowetsky (eds.), *Remaking Canadian Social Policy: Social Security in the Late 1990s*, Halifax: Fernwood Publishing, p. 144.

39. Ibid.

40. Adrie Naylor, 2012, "Economic Crisis and Austerity: The Stranglehold on Canada's Families," *Socialist Project, E-Bulletin* 614, April 9.

41. Ontario Common Front (OCF), 2012, *Falling Behind: Ontario's Backslide into Widening Inequality, Growing Poverty and Cuts to Social Programs,* Toronto: Ontario Common Front, p. 22.

42. Ann Porter, 2003, *Gendered States: Women, Unemployment Insurance and the Political Economy of the Welfare State,* Toronto: University of Toronto Press, p. 212.

43. OCF, 2012, p. 5.

44. Jean Swanson, 2001, *Poor-Bashing: The Politics of Exclusion,* Toronto: Between the Lines.

45. Les Leopold, 2013, "Tennessee: Ayn Rand's Vision of Paradise," *Alternet,* April 12, p. 2.

46. Henry Giroux, 2013, "Violence, U.S.: The Warfare State and the Hardening of Everyday Life," *Monthly Review* 65, 1 (May), p. 46.

47. Frances Fox Piven, 2011, "The War Against the Poor," *TomDispatch,* November 11, p. 1.

48. Christopher Sarlo, 1996, *Poverty in Canada, Second Edition,* Vancouver: Fraser Institute, p. 196.

49. Ibid, p. 2.

Chapter 4: Complex Poverty

1. Oscar Lewis, 1961, *The Children of Sanchez,* New York: Random House, p. 30.

2. Paul Watt, 2008, "Underclass and 'Ordinary People' Discourses: Representing/Re-presenting Council Tenants in a Housing Campaign," *Critical Discourse Studies* 5, 4, p. 346.

3. Charles Murray, 1984, *Losing Ground: American Social Policy 1950–1980,* New York: Basic Books.

4. Elijah Anderson, 1990, *Streetwise: Race, Class and Change in an Urban Community,* Chicago and London: University of Chicago Press, p. 167.

5. Loic Wacquant, 2008, *Urban Outcasts: A Comparative Sociology of Advanced Marginality,* Cambridge, U.K.: Polity Press, p. 271.

6. Michael B. Katz, 1989, *The Undeserving Poor: From the War on Poverty to the War on Welfare,* New York: Pantheon Books, p. 237.

7. C. Wright Mills, 1959, *The Sociological Imagination,* New York: Oxford

University Press, p. 8.

8.   William Julius Wilson, 1987, *The Truly Disadvantaged: The Inner City, The Underclass and Public Policy,* Chicago: University of Chicago Press, p. 14.

9.   Jacqueline Jones, 1993, "Southern Diaspora: Origins of the Northern 'Underclass,'" in Michael B. Katz (ed.), *The Underclass Debate: Views from History,* Princeton: Princeton University Press; Nicholas Lemann, 1991, *The Promised Land: The Great Black Migration and How It Changed America,* New York: Knopf.

10. W.E.B. Dubois, 1899 [1996], *The Philadelphia Negro,* Philadelphia: University of Pennsylvania Press, p. 284.

11. Chicago Commission on Race Relations, 1922, *The Negro in Chicago: A Study of Race Relations and a Race Riot,* Chicago: University of Chicago Press.

12. Kenneth Jackson, 1985, *Crabgrass Frontier: The Suburbanization of the United States,* New York: Oxford University Press.

13. Bennett Harrison and Marcus Weiss, 1998, *Workforce Development Networks: Community-Based Organizations and Regional Alliances,* Thousand Oaks, California: Sage.

14. Richard Freeman and Harry Holzer (eds.), 1986, *The Black Youth Employment Crisis,* Chicago: University of Chicago Press.

15. Loic Wacquant, 2008, p. 3–4.

16. John Hagedorn, 2008, *A World of Gangs: Armed Young Men and Gangsta Culture,* Minneapolis: University of Minnesota Press.

17. Mike Davis, 2006, *Planet of Slums,* London and New York: Verso, p. 13, 17, 19.

18. Ibid, p. 1.

19. Elizabeth Comack, Lawrence Deane, Larry Morrissette and Jim Silver, 2013, *Indians Wear Red: Colonialism, Resistance and Aboriginal Street Gangs,* Halifax and Winnipeg: Fernwood Publishing.

20. See, for example, Sudhir Venkatesh 2006, *Off the Books: The Underground Economy of the Urban Poor,* Cambridge, MA and London: Harvard University Press; Roberta Feldman and Susan Stall, 2004, *The Dignity of Resistance: Women Residents' Activism in Chicago Public*

Housing, Cambridge, U.K.: Cambridge University Press; Rhonda Williams, 2004, *The Politics of Public Housing: Black Women's Struggles Against Urban Inequality,* Oxford: Oxford University Press; bell hooks, 1990, *Race, Gender and Cultural Politics,* Boston: South End Press.

21. Jim Mochoruk with Nancy Kardash, 2000, *The People's Co-op: The Life and Times of a North End Institution,* Halifax and Winnipeg: Fernwood Publishing, p. 5–6; Jim Silver, 2010, "Segregated City: A Century of Poverty in Winnipeg," in Paul Thomas and Curtis Brown (eds.), *Manitoba Politics and Government: Issues, Institutions, Traditions,* Winnipeg: University of Manitoba Press.

22. Alan Artibise, 1975, *Winnipeg: A Social History of Urban Growth 1874–1914,* Montreal: McGill-Queen's University Press.

23. Canada, 1971, *Poverty in Canada: Report of the Special Senate Committee on Poverty,* Ottawa: Minister of Supply and Services, p. xiii–xvi.

24. Ian Adams, William Cameron, Brian Hill and Peter Penz, 1971, *The Real Poverty Report,* Edmonton: Hurtig Publishers, p. v.

25. Jim Harding, 1971, "Canada's Indians: A Powerless Minority," in John Harp and John Hofley (eds.), *Poverty in Canada,* Toronto: Prentice-Hall of Canada.

26. Donald Clairmont and William Magill, 1970, *Nova Scotia Blacks: An Historical and Structural Overview,* Halifax: Institute of Public Affairs, Dalhousie University.

27. See Emile Gosselin, 1971, "The Third Solitude," in John Harp and John Hofley (eds.), *Poverty in Canada,* Toronto: Prentice-Hall of Canada; Urban Social Development Project, 1970, "Social and Mental Health Survey, Montreal, 1966 Summary Report," in W.E. Mann (ed.), *Poverty and Social Policy in Canada,* Toronto: Copp-Clark; W.R. Delagran, 1970, "Life in the Heights," in W.E. Mann (ed.), *Poverty and Social Policy in Canada,* Toronto: Copp Clark.

28, N.H. Lithwick, 1971, *Research Monograph 1: Urban Poverty,* Ottawa: Central Mortgage and Housing Corporation, p. 18; W.R. Delagran, 1970.

29. T.R. Balakrishnan, Paul Maxim and Rozzet Jurdi, 2005, "Social Class versus Cultural Identity as Factors in the Residential Segregation

of Ethnic Groups in Toronto, Montreal and Vancouver for 2001," *Canadian Studies in Population* 32, 2, p. 204–5.

30. For example, see David Ley and Heather Smith, 1997, "Immigration and Poverty in Canadian Cities, 1971–1991," *Canadian Journal of Regional Science* 20.

31. Zoltan Hajnel, 1995, "The Nature of Concentrated Urban Poverty in Canada and the United States," *Canadian Journal of Sociology* 20, p. 514.

32. Eric Fong and Kumiko Shibuya, 2000, "The Spatial Concentration of the Poor in Canadian Cities," *Demography* 37, 4.

33. David Hulchanski, 2002, *Housing Policy for Tomorrow's Cities,* Ottawa: Canadian Policy Research Network, p. 5–6.

34. David Ley and Nicholas Lynch, 2012, *Divisions and Disparities in Lotus-Land: Socio-Spatial Income Polarization in Greater Vancouver, 1970–2005,* Toronto: Cities Centre, University of Toronto.

35. Shauna MacKinnon, 2009, "Manitoba's Poverty Reduction Plan: All Aboard — Destination Unknown," *Fast Facts,* Winnipeg: Canadian Centre for Policy Alternatives-Manitoba; Jim Silver, 2011, *Good Places to Live: Poverty and Public Housing in Canada,* Halifax: Fernwood Publishing.

36. Abdolmohammad Kazemipur and Shiva S. Holli, 2000, *The New Poverty in Canada: Ethnic Groups and Ghetto Neighbourhoods,* Toronto: Toronto Educational Publishing, p. 150–8; David Ley and Heather Smith 1997, p. 36.

37. Abdolmohammad Kazemipur and Shiva S. Holli, 2000, p. 37.

38. Grace-Edward Galabuzi, 2006, *Canada's Economic Apartheid: The Social Exclusion of Racialized Groups in the New Century,* Toronto: Canadian Scholars' Press, p. xi, 182–90.

39. Ibid.

40. David Butler-Jones, 2008, *The Chief Public Health Officer's Report on the State of Public Health in Canada 2008: Addressing Health Inequalities,* Ottawa: Public Health Agency of Canada, p. 17.

41. Steve Pomeroy, 2004, *Moving Forward: Refining the FCM Recommendations for a National Housing Strategy,* Ottawa: Federation of Canadian Municipalities.

42. Mona Shum, Elizabeth Comack, Taz Stuart, Reg Ayre, Stephane Perron, Richard Taki and Tom Kosatsky, 2012, "Bed Bugs and Public Health: New Approaches for an Old Scourge," *Canadian Journal of Public Health* 103, 6.

43. Quoted in Wellesley Institute, 2010, *Precarious Housing in Canada,* Toronto, p. 3.

44. Ian Skelton, 2002, "Residential Mobility of Aboriginal Single Mothers in Winnipeg: An Exploratory Study of Chronic Moving," *Journal of Housing and the Built Environment* 17.

45. Manitoba Health, 1995, *The Health of Manitoba's Children,* Winnipeg: Queen's Printer, p. 107–8.

46. Lars Osberg, 2008, *A Quarter Century of Economic Inequality in Canada: 1981–2006,* Ottawa: Canadian Centre for Policy Alternatives, p. 30–1.

47. Stephen Gaetz, 2012, *The Real Cost of Homelessness: Can We Save Money by Doing the Right Thing?* Toronto: Canadian Homelessness Research Network Press, p. 14.

48. Stephen Gaetz, Jesse Donaldson, Tim Richter and Tanya Gulliver, 2013, *The State of Homelessness in Canada 2013,* Toronto: Canadian Homelessness Research Network Press.

49. Nathan Laurie, 2008, *The Cost of Poverty: An Analysis of the Economic Cost of Poverty in Ontario,* Toronto: Ontario Association of Food Banks, p. 10.

50. Mark Lemstra, Johan Machenbach, Cory Neudorf and Ushasri Nannapaneni, 2009, "High Health Care Utilization and Costs Associated with Lower Socio-Economic Status: Results from a Linked Dataset," *Canadian Journal of Public Health* 100, 3; Marni Brownell, Randy Fransoo and Patricia Martens, 2010, "Social Determinants of Health and the Distribution of Health Outcomes in Manitoba," in Lynne Fernandez, Shauna MacKinnon and Jim Silver (eds.), *The Social Determinants of Health in Manitoba,* Winnipeg: Canadian Centre for Policy Alternatives-Manitoba.

51. Marni Brownell et al. 2010, p. 35–37.

52. Cited in Sonya Gulati, 2013, *Literacy Matters: Unlocking the Literacy Potential of Aboriginal Peoples in Canada,* Toronto: TD Economics,

p. 16.

53. Michael Hart, 2010, "Colonization, Social Exclusion and Indigenous Health," in Lynne Fernandez, Shauna MacKinnon and Jim Silver (eds.), *The Social Determinants of Health in Manitoba,* Winnipeg: Canadian Centre for Policy Alternatives-Manitoba, p. 120, 122.

54. Frances Russell, 2011, "Rich-Poor Gap Speeds up in Canada," *Winnipeg Free Press Online Edition,* September 21.

55. Linda Gionet and Shirin Roshanafshar, 2013, *Select Health Indicators of First Nations People Living Off Reserve, Metis and Inuit,* Ottawa: Statistics Canada, Catalogue No. 82-624-X, p. 9.

56. Lynne Fernandez and Nadine Tonn, 2010, "Food Security as a Social Determinant of Health," in Lynne Fernandez, Shauna MacKinnon and Jim Silver (eds.), *The Social Determinants of Health in Manitoba,* Winnipeg: Canadian Centre for Policy Alternatives-Manitoba, p. 155–56.

57. Michele Ver Ploeg, Vince Breneman, Tracey Farrigan, Karen Hamrick, David Hopkins, Phil Kaufman, Biing-Hwan Lin, Mark Nord, Travis Smith, Ryan Williams, Kelly Kinnison, Carol Olander, Anita Sing and Elizabeth Tuckermanty, 2009, "Access to Affordable and Nutritious Food — Measuring and Understanding Food Deserts and Their Consequences: Report to Congress," Administrative Publication No. (AP-036), USDA, ERS.

58. Food Banks Canada, 2013, *Hunger Count: A Comprehensive Report on Hunger and Food Bank Use in Canada, and Recommendations for Change,* Toronto.

59. Jane Gaskell and Ben Levin, 2012, *Making a Difference in Urban Schools: Ideas, Politics and Pedagogy,* Toronto: University of Toronto Press, p. 12.

60. Iglika Ivanova, 2011, *The Cost of Poverty in B.C.* Vancouver: Canadian Centre for Policy Alternatives-B.C, p. 7.

61. Marni Brownell et al. 2010, p. 40.

62. Sonya Gulati 2013, p. 4, 23.

63. William Julius Wilson 1987, p. 63–92.

64. Ibid, p. 83.

65. Kathryn Edin and Maria Kefalas, 2005, *Promises I Can Keep: Why Poor Women Put Motherhood Before Marriage*, Berkeley, California: University of California Press, p. 205–6.

66. John Hagedorn 2008; Elizabeth Comack et al. 2013.

67. Jim Silver (ed.), 2013, *Moving Forward, Giving Back: Transformative Aboriginal Adult Education*, Halifax: Fernwood Publishing, p. 138.

68. Jim Silver 2011, p. 104–5.

69. Teresa Smith, 2011, "First Nation in Crisis After More Suicides," *Winnipeg Free Press*, September 2.

70. Marni Brownell, 2012, "Time to Treat Kids in Care Differently," *Winnipeg Free Press*, March 22.

71. Carol Sanders, 2013, "Children in Care Perceived as Neglected," *Winnipeg Free Press*, April 30.

72. Jon Gerrard, 2012, "Invest in Families, Not CFS Interventions," *Winnipeg Free Press*, November 19.

73. Yatta Kanu, 2011, *Integrating Aboriginal Perspectives into the School Curriculum: Purposes, Possibilities, and Challenges*, Toronto: University of Toronto Press, p. 12.

74. Bernard Schissel and Terry Wotherspoon, 2003, *The Legacy of School for Aboriginal People: Education, Oppression and Emancipation*, Toronto: Oxford University Press, p. 2.

75. Human Rights Watch, 2013, *Those Who Take Us Away: Abusive Policing and Failures in Protection of Indigenous Women and Girls in Northern British Columbia, Canada*, New York, p. 25–26.

76. Sharene Razack, 2002, "Gendered Racial Violence and Spatialized Justice: The Murder of Pamela George," in Sharene Razack (ed.), *Race, Space and the Law: Unmapping a White Settler Society*, Toronto: Between the Lines; Lisa Priest, 1989, *Conspiracy of Silence*, Toronto: McClelland and Stewart.

77. Amnesty International, 2004, *Stolen Sisters: A Human Rights Response to Discrimination and Violence Against Indigenous Women in Canada*, London, p. 2.

78. Elizabeth Comack, 2012, *Racialized Policing: Aboriginal People's Encounters with the Police*, Halifax and Winnipeg: Fernwood Publishing.

79. Human Rights Watch, 2013, p. 28–29.

80. Elizabeth Comack et al., 2013.

81. Elizabeth Comack and Jim Silver, 2008, "A Canadian Exception to the Punitive Turn? Community Responses to Policing Practices in Winnipeg's Inner City," *Canadian Journal of Sociology* 33, 4.

82. Monica Davey, 2013, "Gun Homocides Ravaging Chicago," *New York Times,* January 6.

83. Elizabeth Comack 2012.

84. Jim Silver 2011, p. 103.

85. Gordon Stephanson, 1957, *A Redevelopment Study of Halifax, Nova Scotia,* Halifax: The Corporation of the City of Halifax, p. 32.

86. Bruktawit Melles, 2003, "The Relationship Between Policy, Planning and Neighbourhood Change: The Case of the Gottingen Street Neighbourhood, 1950–2000," Master of Urban and Rural Planning, Dalhousie University, p. 41.

87. Jim Silver, 2011, p. 103–6.

88. Jim Silver, 2006, *In Their Own Voices: Building Urban Aboriginal Communities,* Halifax: Fernwood Publishing, p. 17–23.

89. John Milloy, 1999, *A National Crime: The Canadian Government and the Residential School System, 1879–1986,* Winnipeg: University of Manitoba Press, p. 42.

90. Howard Adams, 1999, *Tortured People: The Politics of Colonization, Revised Edition,* Penticton, BC: Theytus Books, p. 6.

91. Beverly Daniel Tatum, 1999, *Why Are All the Black Kids Sitting Together in the Cafeteria?* New York: Basic Books, p. 6.

92. Howard Adams, 1999, Introduction.

93. Michael Hart, 2002, *Seeking Mino-Pimatisiwin: An Aboriginal Approach to Helping,* Halifax: Fernwood Publishing, p. 27.

94. Ibid.

95. Ibid, p. 28.

96. Dara Culhane, 2003, "Their Spirits Live Within Us: Aboriginal Women in Downtown Eastside Vancouver," *American Indian Quarterly* 27, 3/4, p. 595.

97. Michelle Alexander, 2010, *The New Jim Crow: Mass Incarceration in the*

Age of Colorblindness, New York and London: The New Press, p. 9.

98. Angela Davis, 2003, *Are Prisons Obsolete?* New York: Seven Stories Press.

99. Loic Wacquant, 2009, *Punishing the Poor: The Neoliberal Government of Social Insecurity,* Durham and London: Duke University Press, p. xv.

100. Michelle Alexander, 2010, p. 184.

101. Ibid, p. 58.

102. Alford Young, 2004, *The Minds of Marginalized Black Men,* Princeton: Princeton University Press, p. 95.

103. Victor Rios, 2011, *Punished: Policing the Lives of Black and Latino Boys,* New York: New York University Press, p. 36.

104. Sonya Gulati, 2013, p. 15.

105. Elizabeth Comack et al., 2013, p. 28–29.

106. Ibid, p. 17.

107. Sonya Gulati, 2013, p. 15.

108. Canadian Centre for Policy Alternatives-Manitoba (CCPA-MB), 2005, *The Promise of Investment in Community-Led Renewal, The State of the Inner City Report 2005, Part Two: A View from the Neighbourhoods,* Winnipeg, p. 24.

109. Jim Silver, 2007, *Unearthing Resistance: Aboriginal Women in the Lord Selkirk Park Housing Developments,* Winnipeg: Canadian Centre for Policy Alternatives-Manitoba.

Chapter 5: The Costs of Poverty

1. Marni Brownell, Randy Fransoo and Patricia Martens, 2010, "Social Determinants of Health and the Distribution of Health Outcomes in Manitoba," in Lynne Fernandez, Shauna MacKinnon and Jim Silver (eds.), *The Social Determinants of Health in Manitoba,* Winnipeg: Canadian Centre for Policy Alternatives-Manitoba; Juha Mikkonen and Dennis Raphael, 2010, *Social Determinants of Health: The Canadian Facts,* Toronto: York University School of Health Policy and Management <http://www.thecanadianfacts.org/>.

2. Cameron Mustard, Morris Barer, Robert Evans, John Horne, Teresa Mayer and Shelley Derksen, 1998, "Paying Taxes and Using Health Care

Services: The Distributional Consequences of Tax Financed Universal Health Insurance in a Canadian Province," Paper presented to the CSLS Conference on the State of Living Standards and the Quality of Life in Canada," Ottawa, October 30–31.

3. Mark Lemstra, Johan Machenbach, Cory Neudorf and Ushasri Nannapaneni, 2009, "High Health Care Utilization and Costs Associated with Lower Socio-Economic Status: Results from a Linked Dataset," *Canadian Journal of Public Health* 100, 3.

4. Iglika Ivanova, 2011, *The Cost of Poverty in B.C.* Vancouver: Canadian Centre for Policy Alternatives-B.C.

5. Ibid.

6. Seth Klein, Marjorie Griffin Cohen, T. Garner, Iglika Ivanova, Marc Lee, Bruce Wallace and Margot Young, 2008, *A Poverty Reduction Plan for BC,* Vancouver: Canadian Centre for Policy Alternatives-BC.

7. Michael Shapcott, 2007, *The Blueprint to End Homelessness in Toronto,* Toronto: Wellesley Institute, p. 1.

8. Ibid, p. 2.

9. Stephen Gaetz, 2012, *The Real Cost of Homelessness: Can we Save Money by Doing the Right Thing?* Toronto: Canadian Homelessness Research Network Press, p. 7.

10. Calgary Homelessness Foundation, 2008, *Report on the Cost of Homelessness in the City of Calgary,* Calgary, p. 2.

11. Michelle Patterson, Julian Somers, Karen Mcintosh, Alan Sheill and Charles James Frankish, 2007, *Housing and Support for Adults with Severe Addictions and/or Mental Illness in British Columbia,* Vancouver: Centre for Applied Research in Mental Health and Addiction, Simon Fraser University, p. 9–11.

12. Michael Shapcott, 2007, *The Blueprint to End Homelessness in Toronto,* Toronto: Wellesley Institute.

13. Steve Pomeroy, 2005, *The Cost of Homelessness: Analysis of Alternative Responses in Four Canadian Cities,* Ottawa: National Secretariat on Homelessness, p. iv.

14. Stephen Gaetz, 2012, p. 10.

15. Quoted in John Stapleton, Brendan Pooran and Rene Doucet, 2011,

Making Toronto Safer: A Cost-Benefit Analysis of Transitional Housing Supports for Men Leaving Incarceration, Toronto: John Howard Society of Toronto, p. 6.

16. Paula Mallea, 2011, *Fearmonger: Stephen Harper's Tough-on-Crime Agenda,* Toronto: James Lorimer, p. 121–23.

17. John Stapleton et al., 2011, p. 2.

18. Bill O'Grady, Stephen Gaetz and Kristy Buccien, 2011, *Can I See Your ID? The Policing of Youth Homelessness in Toronto,* Toronto: Homeless Hub Report Series 5.

19. Paula Goering, Scott Velhuizen, Aimee Watson, Carol Adair, Brianna Kopp, Eric Latimer and Angela Ly, 2012, *At Home/Chez Soi Interim Report,* Ottawa: Mental Health Commission of Canada.

20. Ibid, p. 27.

21. Stephen Gaetz, 2012.

22. Nathan Laurie, 2008, *The Cost of Poverty: An Analysis of the Economic Cost of Poverty in Ontario,* Toronto: Ontario Association of Food Banks, p. 15.

23. Harry Holzer, Diane Whitmore Schanzenbach, Greg Duncan and Jens Ludwig, 2007, *The Economic Costs of Poverty in the United States: Subsequent Effects of Children Growing Up Poor,* Washington, D.C.: Institute for Research on Poverty, Center for American Progress, p. 22.

24. Donald Hirsch, 2008, *Estimating the Costs of Child Poverty,* York, U.K.: The Joseph Rowntree Foundation, p. 1.

25. Stephen Gaetz, Bill O'Grady, Kristy Buccieri, Jeff Karabanow and Allyson Marsolais (eds.), 2013, *Youth Homelessness in Canada: Implications for Policy and Practice,* Toronto: Canadian Homelessness Research Network Press, p. 479.

26. Dina Kulik, Stephen Gaetz, Cathy Crowe and Elizabeth Ford-Jones, 2011, "Homeless Youth's Overwhelming Health Burden: A Review of the Literature," *Paediatric Health Care* 16, 6, p. 43.

27. Catherine Mitchell, 2012, "Child Welfare Looking Like a Black Hole," *Winnipeg Free Press,* December 1.

28. Sonya Gulati, 2013, *Literacy Matters: Unlocking the Literacy Potential of Aboriginal Peoples in Canada,* Toronto: TD Economics, p. 4.

29. Ibid, p. 14.

30. Andrew Sharpe, Jean-Francois Arsenault, Simon Lapointe and Fraser Cowan, 2009, *The Effects of Increasing Aboriginal Educational Attainment on the Labour Force, Output and Fiscal Balance,* Ottawa: Centre for the Study of Living Standards, Research Report 2009-3, p. xi–xiii.

31. Jeffrey Simpson, 2013, "Aboriginal Education Vexes Canada (and Paul Martin)," *Globe and Mail,* May 15.

32. Office of the Correctional Investigator, 2012, *Annual Report of the Office of the Correctional Investigator 2011-2012: IV Aboriginal Issues,* Ottawa.

33. Pathways to Education, n.d. <www.pathwaystoeducation.ca>.

34. Jill Pateman and Ken Coulter, 2009, *Beyond Compassion: Measuring the External Costs of Poverty in Sault Ste. Marie,* Report prepared for the District of Sault Ste. Marie Social Services Administration Board, p. 18–19.

35. Jim Silver (ed.), 2013, *Moving Forward, Giving Back: Transformative Aboriginal Adult Education,* Halifax: Fernwood Publishing, p. 13.

36. Harry Holzer et al., 2007, p. 24.

37. Paul Kershaw, Bill Warburton, Lynell Anderson, Clyde Hertzman, Lori Irwin and Barry Forer, 2010, "The Economic Costs of Early Vulnerability in Canada," *Canadian Journal of Public Health* 101 (Supplement 3), November-December; Healthy Child Manitoba (HCM), Various years, *EDI Provincial Reports* <www.gov.mb.ca/healthy-child/edi/edi_reports.html>.

38. Craig Alexander and Dina Ignjatovic, 2012, *Early Childhood Education Has Widespread and Long-Lasting Benefits,* Toronto: TD Economics Special Report, November 27, p. 8.

39. Canadian Centre for Policy Alternatives (CCPA), 2013, *Alternative Federal Budget 2013: Doing Better Together,* Ottawa, p. 61.

40. Nathan Laurie, 2008, p. 23.

41. Craig Alexander and Dina Ignjatovic, 2012, p. 5.

42. Susan Prentice and Molly McCracken, 2004, *Time for Action: An Economic and Social Analysis of Childcare in Manitoba,* Winnipeg: Child Care Coalition of Manitoba.

43. Martha Friendly and Susan Prentice, 2009, *About Canada: Childcare,* Halifax and Winnipeg: Fernwood Publishing, p. 123.

Chapter 6: Solutions that Work

1. House of Commons (HC) Standing Committee on Human Resources, Skills and Social Development, and the Status of Persons with Disabilities, 2010, *Federal Poverty Reduction Plan: Working in Partnership Toward Reducing Poverty in Canada,* Ottawa: Report of the HUMA Committee, November, p. 249.

2. For details, see <www.canadiansocialresearch.net/anti-poverty.htm>.

3. The elements of the poverty reduction plan described below draw upon, among others: NCW (National Council of Welfare), 2011, *The Dollars and Sense of Solving Poverty,* Ottawa; Canadian Centre for Policy Alternatives-Manitoba (CCPA-MB), 2009, *The View From Here: Manitobans Call for a Poverty Reduction Plan,* Winnipeg; Seth Klein, Marjorie Griffin Cohen, T. Garner, Iglika Ivanova, Marc Lee, Bruce Wallace and Margot Young, 2008, *A Poverty Reduction Plan for BC,* Vancouver: Canadian Centre for Policy Alternatives-BC.

4. See, among many examples of studies identifying these weaknesses, Shauna MacKinnon, 2011, "Poverty Reduction and the Politics of Setting Social Assistance Rates," *Fast Facts,* Winnipeg: Canadian Centre for Policy Alternatives-Manitoba; Stella Lord, 2011, "Let's Make Poverty Reduction a Priority," *Fast Facts,* Halifax: Canadian Centre for Policy Alternatives-Nova Scotia.

5. Ed Broadbent, 2010, *The Rise and Fall of Economic and Social Rights: What Next?* Ottawa: Canadian Centre for Policy Alternatives, p. 8.

6. CCPA-MB, 2009, *The View From Here,* p. 20.

7. Kirsten Bernas and Blair Hamilton, 2013, *Creating Opportunities with Green Jobs: The Story of BUILD and BEEP,* Winnipeg: Canadian Centre for Policy Alternatives-Mb, p. 8.

8. Garry Loewen and Jim Silver, 2007, "Moving Low-Income People into Good Jobs," in John Loxley, Kathleen Sexsmith and Jim Silver (eds.), *Doing Community Economic Development,* Halifax: Fernwood Publishing; Bennett Harrison and Marcus Weiss, 1998, *Workforce Development Networks: Community-Based Organizations and Regional Alliances,* Thousand Oaks, CA: Sage.

9. Ray Silvius and Shauna MacKinnon, 2012, *Making Employment Work: Connecting Multi-Barriered Manitobans to Good Jobs,* Winnipeg: Canadian Centre for Policy Alternatives-Manitoba; Garry Loewen and Jim Silver 2007.

10. Andrew Jackson, 2013, "Minimum Wage Hikes: Benefits Offset the Costs," *Globe and Mail,* March 7; John Schmitt, 2013, *Why Does the Minimum Wage Have No Discernible Effect on Employment?* Washington, D.C.: Center for Economic and Policy Research.

11. *New York Times,* 2013, "From the Bottom Up," February 17.

12. Armine Yalnizyan, 2013, "Study of Income Inequality in Canada—What Can Be Done?" *Presentation to the House of Commons Standing Committee on Finance,* April 30.

13. Iglika Ivanova, 2012, *Working for a Living Wage: Making Paid Work Meet Basic Family Needs in Metro Vancouver,* Vancouver: Canadian Centre for Policy Alternatives-BC.

14. Trish Hennessey, 2012, "What if the Minimum Wage Was a Living Wage?" *Behind the Numbers,* Ottawa: Canadian Centre for Policy Alternatives, p. 1.

15. The methodology for calculating the living wage can be found at <www.policyalternatives.ca/livingwage2012>.

16. Vibrant Communities Calgary, 2012, <www.vibrantcalgary.com/vibrant-initiatives/living-wage/living-wage-basics/>.

17. <www.policyalternatives.ca/sites/default/files/uploads/publications/Saskatchewan Office/2014/01/Living_Wage_for_Regina_2014.pdf>; and <www.policyalternatives.ca/sites/default/files/uploads/publications/BC%20Office/2013/05/2013_Living_Wage_Victoria_Supplement_FINAL.pdf>.

18. Canadian Centre for Policy Alternatives (CCPA), 2013, *Alternative Federal Budget,* Ottawa.

19. CCPA, 2013, p. 60.

20. Martha Friendly and Susan Prentice, 2009, *About Canada: Childcare,* Halifax and Winnipeg: Fernwood Publishing, p. 123.

21. Jim Silver (ed.), 2013, *Moving Forward, Giving Back: Transformative Aboriginal Adult Education,* Halifax: Fernwood Publishing.

22. Ibid, p. 14–15.

23. Ibid, p. 13.

24. Andrew Sharpe, Jean-Francois Arsenault, Simon Lapointe and Fraser Cowan, 2009, *The Effects of Increasing Aboriginal Educational Attainment on the Labour Force, Output and Fiscal Balance,* Ottawa: Centre for the Study of Living Standards, Research Report 2009–3.

25. Errol Black and Jim Silver, 2010, "The Union Makes Us Strong — and Improves Our Health," in Lynne Fernandez, Shauna MacKinnon and Jim Silver (eds.), *The Social Determinants of Health in Manitoba,* Winnipeg: Canadian Centre for Policy Alternatives-Mb, p. 202–3.

26. Andrew Jackson, 2013, "Minimum Wage ...", p. 7.

27. Canadian Labour Congress (CLC), 2013, *The Union Advantage for Young Workers* <www.canadianlabour.ca/about-clc/union-advantage-young-workers>, accessed August 21, 2013.

28. Erroll Black and Jim Silver, 2011, "The Attack on Unions Has Now Come to Canada," *Labour Notes,* Winnipeg: Canadian Centre for Policy Alternatives-Manitoba, April 7.

29. Andrew Jackson, 2013, *Union Communities, Healthy Communities: The New Attack on Unions and its Threat to Shared Prosperity in Canada,* Ottawa: Broadbent Institute, p. 5.

30. Ibid, p. 3.

31. Ibid, p. 12.

32. Garry Sran with Michael Lynk, James Clancy and Derek Fudge, 2013, *Unions Matter,* Ottawa: Canadian Foundation for Labour Rights, p. 1.

33. Erroll Black and Jim Silver, 2011, "The Attack ...."

34. Chris Schenk, 2012, *Unions in a Democratic Society: A Response to the Consultation Paper on the Renewal of Labour Legislation in Saskatchewan,* Ottawa: Canadian Centre for Policy Alternatives, p. 22–23.

35. Juha Mikkonen and Dennis Raphael, 2010, *Social Determinants of Health: The Canadian Facts,* Toronto: York University School of Health Policy and Management <http://www.thecanadianfacts.org/>, p. 54, 56.

36. Steve Pomeroy, 2004, *Moving Forward: Refining the FCM Recommendations for a National Housing Strategy,* Ottawa: Federation of Canadian

Municipalities; Hulchanski, David, 2002, *Housing Policy for Tomorrow's Cities,* Ottawa: Canadian Policy Research Network.

37. CCPA, 2013, p. 97.

38. CCPA, 2013, p. 100–1.

39. John Loxley, 2010, *Aboriginal, Northern and Community Economic Development: Papers and Retrospectives,* Winnipeg: Arbeiter Ring.

40. Jim Silver, 2013.

41. Jim Silver, Molly McCracken and Kate Sjoberg, 2009, *Neighbourhood Renewal Corporations in Winnipeg's Inner City: Practical Activism in a Complex Environment,* Winnipeg: Canadian Centre for Policy Alternatives-Manitoba.

42. Shauna MacKinnon and Sara Stevens, 2008, *Is Participation Having an Impact? Measuring Progress in Winnipeg's Inner City Through the Voices of Community-Based Program Participants,* Winnipeg: Canadian Centre for Policy Alternatives-MB; Jim Silver, 2006, *In Their Own Voices: Building Urban Aboriginal Communities,* Halifax: Fernwood Publishing.

43. Jim Silver, 2011, *Good Places to Live: Poverty and Public Housing in Canada,* Halifax: Fernwood Publishing.

44. NCW (National Council of Welfare), 2011, *The Dollars and Sense of Solving Poverty,* Ottawa, p. 75.

45. Angie-Marie Hancock, 2004, *The Politics of Disgust: The Public Identity of the Welfare Queen,* New York and London: New York University Press.

46. Evelyn Forget, 2011, "The Town With No Poverty: Using Health Administration Data to Revisit Outcomes of a Canadian Guaranteed Annual Income Field Experiment," Paper presented at a Duke University Department of Economics Seminar, April 1, 2011, Available at <econ.duke.edu/events/archive/2011/04/01/history-of-political-economy-lunch-seminar-fri-April-1-2011>.

47. Oscar Lewis, 1969, "The Culture of Poverty," in Daniel Patrick Moynihan (ed.), *On Understanding Poverty,* New York: Basic Books.

48. William Julius Wilson, 1987, *The Truly Disadvantaged: The Inner City, The Underclass and Public Policy,* Chicago: University of Chicago Press, p. 14.

49. Jim Silver, 2011, p. 126.

50. Paul Goldie and Janet McFarland, 2013, "Could 2013 Be the Year We Finally Learn to Love the Taxman?" *Globe and Mail*, January 5.

51. Ed Finn, 2012, "Huge Tax Cuts, Uncollected Taxes Starve our Social Programs, ccpa *Monitor*, July/August, p. 4.

52. Jim Stanford, 2013, "Canada's Tax Cycle Is Turning, and for the Better," *Globe and Mail*, June 7.

53. Ibid.

54. Paul Krugman, 2013, "We Can and Should Raise This Lucky Elite's Taxes," *Globe and Mail*, May 29.

55. Joseph Stiglitz, 2013, "Globalisation Isn't Just About Profits, It's About Taxes Too," *Guardian, United Kingdom*, May 28.

56. Iglika Ivanova and Seth Klein, 2013, *Progressive Tax Options for B.C.: Reform Ideas for Raising New Revenues and Enhancing Fairness*, Vancouver: Canadian Centre for Policy Alternatives-BC, p. 5.

57. Marc Lee and Iglika Ivanova, 2013, *Fairness by Design: A Framework for Tax Reform in Canada*, Ottawa: Canadian Centre for Policy Alternatives, p. 7.

INDEX